# MEMORIES OF CARDIFF'S PAST

# MEMORIES OF CARDIFF'S PAST

DENNIS MORGAN

breedon **books**
PUBLISHING

First published in Great Britain in 2006 by

The Breedon Books Publishing Company Limited

Breedon House, 3 The Parker Centre, Derby, DE21 4SZ.

ISBN 1 85983 505 8

Printed and bound by Cromwell Press, Trowbridge, Wiltshire

# Contents

# Introduction and Acknowledgements

Some years ago I wrote a little book entitled *Discovering Cardiff's Past*. It indicated where various monuments in Cardiff could be found and told the stories which lay behind them. This book is really a sequel to that as I discovered several more plaques, statues and other memorials to the people, places and events which have shaped the city. There is a tendency to regard Cardiff as a modern metropolis, which only became important when its docks were built in the 19th century. While the majority of the stories told in this book date from the last 200 years, I have inserted some earlier topics of interest from the more distant past.

Unfortunately, as I carried out my research, I discovered that some of the plaques, erected by the Cardiff Historical Information Group in the 1980s and 1990s, were in some cases looking the worse for wear and one or two had disappeared altogether. I hope that this book might persuade the powers that be to renew these monuments, which do so much to remind us of the rich and colourful history that is a part of Cardiff's heritage.

I would like to thank those people who have helped me in the writing of this work. I appreciate the assistance given to me by everyone in the Local Studies Department at the Central Library when I was carrying out my research. I would also like to express my gratitude to Mr Matthew Williams, who not only helped me with my research into the Bute family, the West Gate and the Friaries, but also provided me with some previously unpublished photographs.

This reminds me to thank the organisations and individuals who have provided me with so many of my illustrations. Many of them came from the excellent collection in the Central Library or have previously appeared in Stewart Williams's superb series, *Cardiff Yesterday*. Among other contributors are the following:

M. Baldwin, Bill Barrett, BBC Archives Collection, Cardiff Castle Collection, Cardiff City Council, D.R. Carston, J.M. Cronin, Glamorgan Record Office, Harpur-Collins, R.M. Huish, *Ideal Home Magazine*, David Jenkins, J. Geraint Jenkins, Fred Jones, Brian Lee, *London Illustrated News*, Osborne Long, Ian Morgan, Sarah Morgan, National Museum of Wales, W. Penney, Dennis Pope, Popperfoto, Ian Soulsby, Michael Tarver, Chrystal Tilney, Stewart Williams, Welsh Industrial and Maritime Museum, *Western Mail and South Wales Echo,* J.R. Young.

I would like to thank them all and apologise to anyone I have inadvertently omitted. Finally, I must thank my family for the excellent support and encouragement they always give me. In different ways, every one of them has helped me at some stage in the production of this book. If any errors remain, they are my responsibility.

# Chapter 1
# The Third Marquess of Bute

*The statue of the third Marquess of Bute was unveiled in the Friary Gardens in Cathays Park on 16 November 1929. It stands in front of the civic centre, which was to play such an important role in the development of Cardiff.*

JOHN III MARQUESS OF BUTE

John Patrick Crichton Stuart, the third Marquess of Bute, whose statue stands in Cathays Park, was born on 12 September 1847 at Mountstuart House on the Isle of Bute. He was only six months old when his father died. The second Marquess left a massive fortune, based largely on the royalties of the coal mines on his Welsh estates. After his death, young John was brought up by his mother, Sophia. He adored her but his childhood was lonely and almost entirely under female influence. As he later admitted, 'I was kept wrapped up in cotton wool in those days and I did not always like it'.

When Sophia died in 1859, custody of the boy was given to General Charles Stuart, to whom Bute took a dislike. Fortunately for him, Stuart asked the Earl of Galloway to take the lad into his home at Galloway House, and, for the first time, the Marquess was part of a large family circle. He entered Harrow in 1862 and later became a student at Christchurch College in Oxford, where he was described as 'a retiring man who did not mix much with other under-graduates'.

All his life the Marquess was shy and reserved, especially when he was forced to participate in public life. He never made a speech in the House of Lords until 1894 when, as its Rector, he spoke about the affairs of St Andrews University. Those who knew him privately testified to an attractive personality who cared little for London society. He made no attempt to court popularity and, unlike most members of the aristocracy, he had no interest in blood sports. His tastes were 'those of a student and philosopher who lived in a world of his own creation'.

During the 20 years until he reached his majority, the Bute interests in Cardiff were administered by trustees. When the Marquess finally came of age in September 1868, it was a time for great rejoicing in Cardiff. The festivities lasted for a week as special trains brought tenants and well-wishers from the Rhondda, the Vale of Glamorgan and other outposts of the Bute empire in South Wales. There were balloon ascents, concerts, school fetes, regattas, the public roasting of oxen and a magnificent fireworks display. A triumphal arch was erected in Crockerton Street and, when the Marquess visited Cardiff, an expensive temporary building was erected in the castle forecourt. The entire celebration cost

*The* Illustrated London News *shows the jubilant scenes in Crockerton Street as crowds gather and the flags come out to mark the coming of age of the Marquess in 1868. The triumphal arch indicates the powerful position the Bute family held in Cardiff at that time.*

the estate £14,000. When the young nobleman spoke at a banquet given in his honour, he made a promise to the 3,000 guests: 'When I come into this great and growing town and see the vast numbers of men who are nourished by its prosperity... I feel the ties of duty to them which bind me... I mean to try to do my very best for this place to the end of my life'.

While he was at Oxford, the Marquess, after deep thought and study, became a convert to the Roman Catholic faith, though he did not publicly proclaim it until a few months after his coming of age. The news came as a profound shock both in Cardiff and his native Scotland. Both his parents had been staunch Protestants and yet, by the time of his death, the name of Bute was so synonymous with the Catholic faith that many people assumed it had always been the religion of the family.

On the Isle of Bute the local newspaper commented on the Marquess's 'perversion to Rome' and the effect on the local community. The people of the island were so bitter that they turned his portrait to the wall and even took pot shots at it. In an age when religious passions ran high, the news also shocked the majority of people in Cardiff, though there was a sizeable Catholic minority, mainly Irish immigrants, who were delighted with his decision.

Henceforth religion became the inspiration of Bute's life, influencing virtually everything he did. He loved its ritual and was a leading figure among lay Catholics

at the Vatican Council. Benjamin Disraeli, who met the Marquess when he came of age and later attended his wedding, made him the central figure in his most successful novel, *Lothair*.

Bute was among the most eligible bachelors in Britain when he left Oxford, and it was natural that he should marry into a Catholic family. His bride was Gwendoline Fitzalan-Howard, eldest daughter of Lord Howard of Glossop. Her grandfather was the Duke of Norfolk, head of the leading Catholic family in Britain. After their marriage at Brompton Oratory in April 1872, Lord and Lady Bute spent their honeymoon at Cardiff Castle. The occasion was once again

*No expense was spared in the celebrations of 1868. This splendid banqueting hall was part of a temporary structure at the castle, which also included a ballroom and reception rooms.*

*A typical portrait of the Marquess, showing him in thoughtful mood. Scholarly and deeply religious, he did not enjoy the public duties which were an inevitable part of life for such an important figure.*

The arch erected in High Street for the visit of the Marquess and his bride shortly after their wedding in 1872. Just in front of it is the statue of the second Marquess of Bute.

Lady Gwendolen with three of her children, Margaret, Ninian and John. The family are preparing for the Coronation of Edward VII in 1902. John was now the fourth Marquess of Bute, following the death of his father two years earlier.

an opportunity for great celebrations in the borough. A splendid triumphal arch was erected in High Street and details of the marriage occupied 30 columns in the *Western Mail*.

The Butes had four children. Their only daughter, Margaret, was born in 1875 and she was followed by three boys. All three were educated at Harrow, despite the fact that the Marquess had few happy memories of his own schooldays there. The eldest, named John in accordance with the family tradition, was born in 1881 and succeeded his father to become the fourth Marquess. Ninian, whose statue stands in the Gorsedd Gardens, was born in 1883. He became MP for Cardiff in 1910 and was killed at the Battle of Loos in World War One. Colum, the youngest of Bute's sons, was born in 1886.

In the mid-19th century Cardiff was a growing industrial town with few cultural merits. Not surprisingly, it held few attractions for a man of Bute's artistic temperament. Usually he spent about six weeks of the year in Cardiff, and his long absences from the area, where his wealth was based, led to criticism. The Marquess loved to travel, especially to the glories of the ancient world in the Mediterranean. As he once admitted, 'Athens and Assisi have spoilt me for anything else'. He was never happier than when he visited Palestine, where he bought an estate.

As the fortune he inherited showered forth its wealth, the Marquess became one of the richest men in Britain. Despite his fabulous riches, he showed little interest in acquiring money which, as the *Western Mail* wrote in his obituary, 'flowed into his coffers unbidden and unsought'. When the Marquess came of age, he had no great enthusiasm for commerce and industry and was prepared to leave the administration of his estate in South Wales, especially the docks at Cardiff, to W.T. Lewis. This tough, hard-headed businessman, who had left school at the age of 12, later became Lord Merthyr. However, Bute could not completely avoid dealing with the problems created by the extraordinary expansion of the Welsh coal industry. As Cardiff became the greatest coal-exporting port in the world, new docks were essential.

At the same time, the docks made little profit and proved a disappointing investment for the Bute family. The earlier docks became obsolete as vessels became larger, the cost of building them always exceeded estimates and charges to the users were always subject to Parliamentary approval. The Marquess agreed to the building of the Roath Basin in 1874 but showed a reluctance to extend the docks any further. He was only persuaded to build the Roath Dock after Lewis, now a prominent industrialist in his own right, argued that a further dock must be built to meet the needs of the coal trade. The cutting of the first sod in 1883 was marked, as Bute occasions always were, with a public holiday and a procession.

When Bute was given permission by Parliament to raise the charges at the docks, there was uproar. David Davies of Llandinam, founder of the Ocean Coal

*The Marquess
performing two public
duties in Cardiff. In the
upper photograph he is
laying the foundation
stone for the infirmary,
and in the lower he is
setting in motion the
steam hammer as work
commences on the
Roath Dock.*

Company, was a pioneer in the construction of Barry Docks and forecast that this would lead to grass growing on the streets of Cardiff. He was wrong. There was plenty of trade for everyone, but Bute was forced to plan one final dock at a cost of £2.5 million to accommodate the largest ships of the day and maintain Cardiff's industrial prosperity.

The Marquess never lived to see the opening of the Queen Alexandra Dock in 1907, and, till the end of his days, he was looking for ways of terminating his interest in the port. It is ironic that much of his wealth from mineral royalties was diverted to his 'white elephant' at the docks. He resented the unjust accusations that he was making exorbitant profits from them, when in fact the reverse was the case and the Bute Docks were really a non-profit making public service.

Unlike his father, Bute made no great impact on the political life of Cardiff. Though he considered himself a Conservative and made substantial donations to the party, he never took an active interest in politics. He wrote to a friend, 'I suppose I may call myself... an old-fashioned Tory'. While he launched the *Western Mail* in 1869 as a means of promoting the Conservative cause, he never tried to influence its content and it was not long before he sold it.

While Bute had little interest in politics and economics, in the spheres of building and town planning he was to make a major contribution towards creating the attractive city that Cardiff is today. He continued his father's policy of purchasing land in and around the town, and by the late 19th century the Bute Estate had acquired 22,000 acres of land in South Wales. Added to his holdings

elsewhere, this made the estate one of the largest in Britain. Streets and parks named after the Butes appear throughout Cardiff. Some of them have a connection with the second Marquess, but many are associated with the third Marquess and his family. Fitzalan Place, Howard Gardens and Glossop Terrace take their names from his wife, while Lady Margaret's Terrace, Ninian Park, Ninian Road and Colum Road are named after his children.

Where the Bute Estate could control development, the trustees and later the Marquess did their best to ensure that it was carried out tastefully. They did not always succeed, but Windsor Place, Park Place and Cathedral Road remain among the finest Victorian streets in Britain. In the suburbs, the area around Roath Park is a superb example of 19th-century architecture. The creation of squares or gardens, such as those in Riverside and Grangetown, reflect Bute's ideas on town planning and were intended to create a breathing space amid the growth of

*The original* Western Mail *offices in St Mary Street. Though Lord Bute founded the newspaper, he was never really interested in it. Within a few years he disposed of the paper to its editor, Lascelles Carr.*

15

urbanisation. For this reason, Cardiff Arms Park was also reserved for recreational purposes.

In 1887 the Marquess presented the Corporation with 103 acres of land, valued at £50,000, on which most of Roath Park was built. His generosity was not universally acclaimed. There were always voices antagonistic towards the Butes because of the influence they wielded in Cardiff. Some members of the council claimed the land was no more than a 'malarial bog', so far from the town no one would want to visit it. The Ratepayers' Association argued there was no justification for spending huge sums on Roath Park, since the improvement would merely enrich Bute and other landowners as they developed the surrounding land.

Fortunately for the people of Cardiff, the council went ahead and created the splendid park and lake enjoyed by so many today. The opening ceremony was performed by the Marquess and his son, the Earl of Dumfries, on 20 June 1894. It was the young Earl's 13th birthday and, after driving along gaily decorated streets from the town centre, it was he who had the honour of declaring Roath Park officially open.

To the west of the castle, Bute preserved an open space, unsurpassed in the heart of any British city apart from London. During the 19th century the Marquess often received tempting offers to develop Bute Park but, as he did not need the money, he refused them all. Similarly, he rejected any attempts to build on farms he owned at Pontcanna and Blackweir. The people of Cardiff became the beneficiaries of his wisdom in 1947, when the fifth Marquess presented the castle and Bute Park as a gift to the city. Within five minutes of entering the park, people find a haven of

*The pleasure gardens at Roath Park in the Edwardian age. The Marquess contributed most of the land on which this splendid park, enjoyed by the people of Cardiff for more than 100 years, was constructed.*

peace away from the noise of traffic, and it is possible to walk two miles through beautiful countryside as far as Western Avenue.

The restoration of Cardiff Castle was Bute's greatest architectural triumph. He met the brilliant if somewhat eccentric architect William Burges at Oxford in 1865, and soon afterwards the Marquess commissioned him to restore the castle. The two men became good friends, and Bute commented on one occasion 'Burges is very clever and his company is amusing which is always a luxury'. The architect's humorous personality captivated Lady Gwendolen, who commented 'Ugly Burges, who designs lovely things. Isn't he a duck'! For Burges it was an architect's dream as he had no restraints in terms of money and his patron shared his romantic idealism of the mediaeval Gothic age. As Bute said, 'I have a considerable taste for art and archaeology and happily the means to indulge them'.

While Burges used his riotous imagination to create an exuberant Victorian extravaganza, the Marquess did not hesitate to scrutinise his plans in detail and demand amendments where he saw fit. He often backed his suggestions with his own sketches and examined 10 different designs for the Clock Tower before he was satisfied. The lions on the Animal Wall were returned for alteration as they were, 'too modest in demeanour, savouring rather of pets than of roaring lions'.

*The remains of the Blackfriars Church can be seen in this view of Bute Park at the height of summer. The park is another legacy from the Marquess that the people of Cardiff are able to enjoy today.*

*William Burges was one of the great Victorian architects. At the same time his love of rich decoration and furnishing made him very expensive to employ. The Marquess was one of the few who could afford him.*

*Burges transformed the west wall of the castle. The spire of the Octagonal Tower was an addition to the mediaeval building, but, of the new towers, the most important was the magnificent Clock Tower. The clock and the rich statuary surrounding it have recently been restored.*

The existing Octagonal and Herbert Towers were retained along the west wall and three new towers were added, the most impressive of which is the Clock Tower. Inside the castle the full glory of Burges's work is reflected. The Bute workshops in Cardiff and London employed the finest craftsmen from Britain and abroad to fashion masterpieces in wood, gold, marble and stone. Some of the rooms appear rather small but all are richly decorated. The themes reflect Bute's personality and interests in mediaeval history, the Middle East, the occult and of course his devout religious beliefs.

The Arab Room was intended to be a faithful replica of a room in a Sultan's palace, though the final product was a creation of the Bute workshops. Another room in the Octagonal Tower is devoted to the works of Geoffrey Chaucer. At the summit of the Bute Tower is a splendid roof garden, where the Marquess liked to spend much of his time contemplating and reading works of theology. The lower level of the Mediaeval Hall was converted into a library and drawing room, but the upper storey became the Banqueting Hall, perhaps the most beautiful room in the castle. Its stained-glass windows depict the mediaeval Lords of Glamorgan, while the overmantel of its fireplace and the murals on the walls portray the life and times of Robert the Consul. As Lord of Glamorgan, he gave Cardiff its first town charter.

The Banqueting Hall as it appeared when the castle was one of the many residences belonging to the Butes. It shows Burges's creativity at its most exuberant. The splendid hammerbeam roof displays the coat of arms of the Bute ancestors.

Memories of the past were faithfully retained as Bute made a detailed study of the castle's history. His interest in archaeology led to the rediscovery and careful preservation of the Roman Wall. Likewise, the Norman Keep was left unspoilt as a reminder of the days when it was the stronghold of the Lords of Glamorgan. The sites of the two friaries were cleared of debris and then excavated before being clearly marked out.

The Marquess restored a number of other castles throughout Britain and at Tongwynlais, a few miles north of Cardiff, Burges was employed to renovate the ruins of Castell Coch. The result was a picturesque fairytale castle with conical towers. Built as a summer retreat, Bute rarely used it. Set in attractive woodland above the Taff, Castell Coch has become a popular location for film and television producers. Bute attempted to cultivate vines on its slopes and for many years this was the only commercial vineyard in Britain.

The Marquess was a patriotic Scot whose favourite home was at Mountstuart House on the Isle of Bute. After the original house was largely destroyed by fire in 1877, he rebuilt it in an Italian Gothic style at a cost of £600,000. He also published the *Scottish Review*, advocating Home Rule for Scotland, and his educational endowments in Scotland amounted to £250,000. As these were paid from his investments in Glamorgan, they caused some resentment in Wales.

However, Bute's donations to good causes in Cardiff and Glamorgan were substantial. He paid off the debt of the old Cardiff Infirmary and provided the site for its replacement at Longcross. He gave £13,000 towards the rebuilding of the Hamadyrad Hospital and, as President of University College, he contributed

£10,000 towards its funds. One of his more touching endowments was the 'Bute Dowry', established by him on the occasion of his silver wedding. The annual income from the original gift of £1,000 was to be 'given to some girl of poorer classes whose marriage might be impeded by the want of such a sum'.

Bute's religious beliefs ensured that Catholic charities such as Nazareth House and the Convent of the Good Shepherd benefitted from his generosity. He contributed towards the building of St David's Church in Charles Street, which later became the seat of the Roman Catholic Archbishop of Wales. Yet the Marquess was no bigot. He helped to restore a number of historic Anglican churches, such as St John's in Cardiff, and granted generous leases to help the Jews build their synagogues.

Bute's enthusiasm for Celtic culture and traditions was also reflected in Wales.

*Opposite page: Castell Coch, the 'Red Castle', was originally built in the 13th century by Gilbert de Clare to protect the river crossing near Tongwynlais. From its ruins, Burges created this beautiful little castle which would not look out of place on the Rhine.*

*When St David's Cathedral was built, the Marquess, as Cardiff's leading Roman Catholic, made a generous donation towards its construction. Its solid Gothic structure was planned by Pugin and Pugin, the firm that designed the Houses of Parliament in 1834.*

21

*The Marquess in his robes as Mayor of Cardiff. He was the first nobleman to be the mayor of a large borough for 200 years, and his year of office was generally regarded as a success.*

He used his extraordinary flair for languages to make himself fluent in Welsh and ensured that all his children learnt the language. At the Cardiff National Eisteddfod in 1882, his defence of the Welsh tongue led to the foundation of the Welsh Language Society. The Marquess accepted office as chairman or president of a number of organisations in Cardiff, although owing to the limited amount of time he spent in the town his participation in their affairs was minimal.

When the Corporation invited Bute to serve as Mayor of Cardiff in November 1890, he only agreed after pointing out that his commitments would restrict him to being no more than a figurehead. His readiness to be of service was a real sacrifice in view of his shy, retiring temperament, which made it an ordeal to address public meetings. He spent money lavishly, and at the end of his year in office he presented the Corporation with a magnificent loving cup, which still has a place of distinction among the city's regalia. For his part, Bute was obviously pleased with the honour bestowed on him. It may have been this accolade that led him to make the most important decision he ever took in the affairs of the borough.

When the council accepted Bute's offer of a site in Cathays Park for a new civic centre, he imposed strict conditions on the way it was to be developed. He stipulated how the avenues should be laid out and the trees preserved. There were to be no commercial buildings and the area was to be exclusively retained for civic, cultural and educational purposes. The result of Bute's foresight was his most significant legacy to Cardiff, as Cathays Park blossomed into one of the finest civic centres in the world, the envy of every other city in Britain.

The City Hall is an architectural gem and over the years other splendid

buildings have made their bow. The offer of a site in Cathays Park attracted the National Museum of Wales to Cardiff to 'teach the world about Wales and the Welsh people about their fatherland'. Most of the other buildings in Cathays Park are the property of the university but, in addition to an array of impressive architecture, there are ample open spaces. The Gorsedd Gardens and Queen Alexandra Gardens are adorned with beautiful flower beds, interesting statues and other memorials.

*A family takes a stroll among the flowers of the future King Edward VII Avenue in Cathays Park. It is 1900 and two more years will pass before work begins on the civic centre.*

The largest building in Cathays Park is the Welsh Office, from which so many decisions affecting everyday life in the Principality are taken. When the Welsh local councils were invited to choose a capital for Wales in 1954, the choice was overwhelmingly in favour of Cardiff, almost certainly because its civic centre reflected so many aspects of Welsh life.

Sadly, the Marquess never lived to see the fruits of his vision. He became ill in 1899 and lingered for more than a year before he died on 9 October 1900 at Dumfries House in Ayrshire. He was buried in the chapel by the foreshore at his beloved Mountstuart House. A few days later his wife and children travelled to Jerusalem to bury his heart, as he had always wished, on the Mount of Olives.

The Scottish family from the Isle of Bute exercised an enormous influence over

*The chapel by the seashore at Mountstuart House, where the third Marquess of Bute was laid to rest. Outside the chapel a Celtic cross symbolises his links with Scotland and Wales.*

Cardiff in the 19th century. Both the second and the third Marquess were true 'city fathers' who paved the way for Cardiff to grow from a small Victorian town to a great city. The second Marquess is often referred to as 'the father of modern

Cardiff, but, when we look at Roath Park, Bute Park, the castle and the civic centre, we realise how much the city owes to the vision and perception of the third Marquess.

**Further reading:**

**Davies, J.** *Cardiff and the Marquesses of Bute*, University of Wales Press, 1981.
**Morgan, D.** *The Cardiff Story*, Dennis Morgan, 1991.

*Cardiff's civic centre before World War Two. In the foreground, left to right, are the Law Courts, the City Hall and the National Museum. Behind the War Memorial is the Welsh Board of Health, which later became the Welsh Office.*

## *Chapter 2*
# The Docksmen

In the 19th century, Welsh coal fuelled the industries of the world and the Cardiff Docks were built to export that coal. The second Marquess of Bute built the first of them in 1839, and, as the century went on, further docks were built to meet the insatiable demand. From 1860 onwards steamers from Cardiff 'tramped' the world with their cargoes of black diamonds and by 1910 there were 367 of these sturdy vessels operating from the docks. There are several memorials in Cardiff to the coal and shipping magnates who were known as the docksmen. More recently a well-deserved statue has been erected to the miners whose labours contributed to the growth of Cardiff. Plaques have also been placed on the buildings associated with those exciting days before World War One when it seemed that the lucrative profits made from coal would last forever.

*One of the early tramp steamers that made Cardiff famous all over the world. As the 19th century took its course, these sturdy vessels became ever larger to meet the demand for Welsh coal.*

A small capital was enough to enter the shipping business and companies were often formed with a single ship, purchased on mortgage. An advertisement offering to carry a cargo of coal overseas might be placed at the Coal Exchange or in the local newspaper. In anticipation of a handsome profit, there was no shortage of investors prepared to buy shares in the vessel for its maiden voyage. If the market was buoyant, they could expect a handsome dividend, although if the price of coal fell the small investor was liable to lose their money. The system was a satisfactory way of allowing someone with limited means to go into the shipping business. Even when companies prospered and owned several vessels, each ship might be registered as a separate company, thereby restricting any liability to that ship only. There were unscrupulous characters who avoided even the slightest risk to themselves by imposing concealed charges on their investors. Even worse, some of them embezzled their investors' money without ever putting to sea at all.

*The Welsh miners helped to make Cardiff the greatest coal exporting port in the world. The statue overlooking the Roath Basin is a recognition of their part in creating the prosperity of the city.*

J. Kyrle Fletcher wrote that the docksmen 'combine the caution of a Scot with the shrewdness of the Tynesider, and the cunning of the devil himself'. Undoubtedly many of them were extroverts. Charles Stallybrass was born in Siberia. He was the son of a missionary, and among his claims to fame was the translation of the Bible into Mongolian. He came to Cardiff in 1857 and within 20 years he owned five tramp steamers.

Another interesting character was Antonio Leonardo Trifone, Count de Lucovich. Born in 1832 in Dalmatia, he traced his noble ancestry back many centuries, but, despite the opposition of his family, he decided to enter the world of commerce rather than law. In 1850 he arrived at Cardiff, and it was not long before he earned a reputation as one of the most colourful characters at the docks. He registered his five vessels, all of them with Italian names, at Trieste and concentrated his trade in the Adriatic, an area with which he was familiar.

Many of the docksmen came from humble beginnings. William Seager, whose

*So crowded was the shipping at Cardiff Docks in the late 19th century, that one observer claimed it was possible to walk from one side of the East Dock to the other without getting your feet wet.*

*Antonio Leonardo Trifone, Count de Lucovich, was a man of distinguished appearance. With a flowing beard reaching down to his chest, he soon became an impressive figure at the docks in the mid-Victorian era.*

family came from Devon, started his working life on a wage of 4s a week in a ship chandlery. He saved enough to become a ship chandler himself, and after making wise investments he bought his first ship, the *Tempus*, in 1904. Seager was cautious in building up his company, and in 1914 he possessed four vessels, all of them less than 10 years old.

Evan Thomas from Aberporth and Daniel Radcliffe of Merthyr formed one of the largest Cardiff shipping firms. Neither of them had much money when they purchased their first ship in 1882, but within 10 years they had 15 new tramp steamers. Their success was largely due to their ability to raise capital. Evan Thomas's brother-in-law was a shareholder and a bank manager in Dolgellau who used his position to persuade customers to buy shares in the shipping firm.

An even more notable sponsor for the firm was a Nonconformist minister, J. Cynddylan Jones from Cardiganshire. Evan Thomas paid him two percent of the company's profits in the 1880s, so not surprisingly Cynddylan exhorted his congregation to enjoy an earthly reward by investing in the company. One newspaper reporter somewhat cynically observed: 'He deserves to be appointed chaplain to the fleet'.

One of the shrewdest of these entrepreneurs was W.J. Tatem, who was born at Appledore in Devon in 1868. He spent some time at sea, but at the age of 18, after being shipwrecked and suffering a bout of 'Yellowjack', he decided to learn the shipping business. He joined Anning Brothers, a firm of local shipowners, and by 1897 he had saved enough to purchase his first ship, the *Lady Lewis*. It was the beginning of his rise to fortune as he invested in the new, larger type of steamer. Within 10 years Tatem was a millionaire, with 16 single-ship companies trading in South America and the Mediterranean.

By some, Tatem was labelled as 'ignorant, rough and uncouth'. He was said to have committed the unpardonable error of turning his back on the King and Queen when they opened the Queen Alexandra Dock in July 1907. Possibly such comments arose from sour grapes. There is little doubt that he was happy to flaunt his wealth, but on that same day he showed how capable he was of kindness as he set aside two of his ships for disabled children to view the proceedings. Later he provided them with a very good tea at his country home.

*J. Cynddylan Jones who, despite his appearance of benevolent piety, showed a shrewd financial sense in promoting the merits of investing in the shipping firm of Evan Thomas and Radcliffe.*

*SS* Torrington *was a typical tramp steamer, which helped to make the fortune of W.J. Tatem. The ship was torpedoed in April 1917, and its crew were lined up on the deck of the U-boat. All of them except the master were drowned when the U-boat crash-dived without warning.*

*The* City of Cardiff, *the first vessel purchased by Sir William Reardon-Smith. This was its untimely end when the ship was wrecked during a gale at Mill Bay near Lands End on 11 March 1912.*

Tatem's first vessel was captained by William Reardon-Smith. He too came from Appledore and went to sea as a cabin boy at the age of 12. He became a master mariner who had many commands before he retired from the sea in 1900. Five years later he bought his first ship, the *City of Cardiff*. It was the beginning of a famous shipping line which by 1922 numbered 39 vessels.

Richard and John Cory were born in Devon but made their fortune in South Wales. Their father, also named Richard, was the owner of a small vessel trading between Cardiff, Bristol and Ireland. In 1838 he opened a ship chandler's store near Custom House Street, but, as the coal industry grew, he enlarged his business and moved to the docks. When Richard the elder retired in 1859, he and his two sons had built up a flourishing business. With their interests as ship owners, coal merchants, colliery agents and exporters, Cory Brothers and Company took full advantage of the opening of the Suez Canal. They developed 118 depots and agencies throughout the world to distribute coal supplied from their own collieries in the Rhondda, Aberdare and Neath valleys.

Related to the Cory brothers was John Cory from Padstow. He already had a successful business when he came to Cardiff in 1872, and by the end of the century the firm had 23 ships trading in coal exports and imports of iron ore and timber. In 1898 they built the impressive offices that still occupy the corner of Mountstuart Square and James Street.

These were a few of the docksmen who made and sometimes lost a fortune. In 1912 there were at least 20 millionaires trading at the Coal and Shipping

Exchange, more per head of population than anywhere else in Britain. They were sometimes described as buccaneers because of the cut-throat nature of their business and their readiness to take a gamble. Yet, in the process of acquiring their wealth and contributing to the growth of Cardiff, many of the docksmen became generous donors to local charities.

*The substantial offices of the Cory Brothers still stand at the junction of Bute Place and Bute Street, but their great days as the headquarters of one of Cardiff's leading shipping and coal companies are long gone.*

*The Cory Hall in Station Terrace was a notable landmark in Cardiff until its demolition in 1987. Built by John Cory on behalf of the Temperance Movement, this photograph shows how it looked in 1912.*

*The famous Cardiff sculptor Sir William Goscombe John, designed the statue of John Cory that stands in the Gorsedd Gardens in Cathays Park. Erected during his lifetime, it was a tribute to a great philanthropist.*

The Cory brothers were both devout Christians and gave generously to good causes, especially the Temperance Movement and the Salvation Army. John is particularly remembered for his generosity to the Sailors' Rest in Butetown, Dr Barnardo's Homes and the original Cardiff YMCA. He built the Cory Hall in Station Terrace in memory of his father, and for several years it was the home of the Cardiff Temperance movement. Opened in 1896, it also served as a venue for public meetings. John Cory's bronze statue in the Gorsedd Gardens is a recognition of the high regard in which he was held by the people of Cardiff.

Sir William Reardon-Smith died in 1935 at the age of 79 and his memory is honoured at the City Hall. During his lifetime he gave away more than £150,000 to colleges, hospitals and orphanages and supervised the collection of £100,000 for the National Museum of Wales, which named its lecture theatre in his honour. At the end of World War One he established the Reardon-Smith Nautical College in Fairwater, where 30 boys were admitted every year for a three-year course leading to the prospect of a successful naval career. Sadly the college closed after the collapse of the firm in 1985.

William Tatem, whose wartime services earned him a peerage as Lord Glanely of St Fagans, was given the freedom of Cardiff in 1928 in recognition of his generosity to philanthropic causes. Among these was his contribution towards the Tatem Physics and Chemistry Laboratories at Cardiff University, which were opened by the Prince of Wales in 1930.

For many years the docksmen conducted their business in the open streets or, if the weather was unkind, in one of the many public houses near the docks. In 1874 a regular meeting place was established at the Mercantile Club, a building which no longer exists. The club was open from 10 in the morning until eight at night and, in the process of transacting business, it offered hospitality similar to gentlemen's clubs in London.

By the 1880s the growth of the port required a more permanent venue, and the Marquess of Bute gave his approval for the construction of the Coal and Shipping Exchange in Mountstuart Square. A plaque records the importance of this building in the maritime history of Cardiff. Built in a combination of Gothic and Classical styles, the design was originally submitted as a pen-and-ink sketch by Edwin Seward. It met with the approval of the Marquess and the Exchange was built at a cost of £40,000. It was erected on the gardens in the centre of Mountstuart Square and was formally opened for business in February 1886.

On the occasion of the King and Queen's visit to open the Queen Alexandra Dock, the *Western Mail* commented 'On the floor of the Cardiff

*This bust of Sir William Reardon-Smith stands in the Marble Hall of the City Hall. He was another docksman who, after making his fortune, contributed to many generous causes which benefitted the people of Cardiff.*

*The Reardon-Smith Theatre was named after Sir William in recognition of his work on behalf of the National Museum of Wales. The attractive semi-circular building is a popular venue for concerts and educational lectures.*

*The plaque at the Coal Exchange was erected by the Cardiff Historical Information Group. The picture of the Exchange clock is significant as it reminded traders of the times of Cardiff's high tides.*

THE EXCHANGE

THE COAL AND SHIPPING EXCHANGE WAS OPENED IN 1886,
FOUNDED BY THE MERCANTILE CLUB OF 1874 THIS HISTORIC PLACE,
BUILT ON THE SITE OF AN OLD GARDEN, WAS TO BECOME THE
COMMERCIAL CENTRE OF CARDIFF AND NEIGHBOURING PORTS
HOUSING THE STOCK EXCHANGE AND WITH A WORLDWIDE TRADE
IN COAL IRON AND STEEL CARRIED BY THE GREAT FLEETS OF
CARDIFF OWNED SHIPS.
PRIOR TO 1886 BUSINESS WAS EXCHANGED ON THE BUSY OPEN
STREETS AROUND PIER-HEAD UNLESS, IT WAS SAID, INCLEMENT
WEATHER DROVE THE MAGNATES TO CONTINUE THEIR TRANSACTIONS
IN THE LOCAL HOSTELRIES. IN 1911 WHEN THE EXCHANGE WAS
CLOSED FOR ALTERATIONS, SOME FIFTEEN HUNDRED MEMBERS
ONCE MORE RESORTED TO THE OPEN AIR AND THE FORECOURT
BECAME "THE FLOOR".
GREAT DRAMAS WERE ENACTED WITHIN THESE WALLS
PERHAPS NONE SO MOVING AS ON THE 16 JULY 1913 WHEN
A WELCOME WAS GIVEN TO THE OFFICERS AND CREW
OF CAPTAIN SCOTT'S ANTARCTIC EXPEDITION SHIP,

"TERRA NOVA"

"WITHOUT THE ASSISTANCE GIVEN BY
CARDIFF, THIS EXPEDITION WOULD
NOT HAVE BEEN POSSIBLE"

Donated by Cllr. C.H. Rapport. M.B.E. C.St.J. J.P.

Exchange, everyone who is anyone will be found about noon every day'. This was the peak time for trading and deals, involving perhaps the sale of £50,000 worth of coal, would be settled with a handshake.

In 1912 the Exchange was extended by E. Turner and Sons to become the largest building in Cardiff Bay. A photograph, taken when it was reopened, shows the docksmen rubbing shoulders with one another, while onlookers are surveying the floor from the balconies. The new Exchange contained 120 suites of offices, a post and telegraph office, a wine merchant, tailor, tobacconist shop and a barber. So it was possible for these tycoons to celebrate a successful deal with a bottle of champagne, have their hair cut or take the opportunity to be measured for a new suit, without ever having to take their eyes

*The Exchange was the hub of the commercial life of the docks. In this view, taken before World War One, the extended ladders on the left indicate the scale of the building.*

OPENING OF NEW CARDIFF EXCHANGE

FEBRUARY 20th 1912

CARD No 3

A & G Taylor 59, QUEEN ST CARDIFF.

off the activity on the floor. In the basement of the Exchange, Culley's Restaurant offered good food and a place to relax after the morning's business.

The Pier Head Building was a familiar sight for seamen returning to Cardiff after a long voyage and is another magnificent building recalling Cardiff's maritime past. Designed by William Frame to provide offices for the Bute Dock Company, it was formally opened on August Bank Holiday 1897. Frame had assisted William Burges in the renovation of Cardiff Castle and Castell Coch and the love of Gothic architecture they shared is shown in the magnificent skyline of the Pier Head Building. Hexagonal chimneys, pinnacled turrets and gargoyles culminate in a superb castellated tower. The interior is equally splendid and is reminiscent of the restoration work at the castle. Until 1998 the Pier Head Building was used as the headquarters for the ports of South Wales and it now serves as the visitors' centre for the National Assembly.

The docksmen continued to prosper during World War One, despite an excess profits tax, as the price of coal soared to new levels. Though the merciless U-boat campaign sent many of their ships and their gallant crews to the bottom of the sea, the shipping magnates were compensated for every vessel they lost. Evan Thomas and Radcliffe alone lost 20 of its 28 ships in World War One. Yet the company

*When the Exchange reopened in 1912, the docksmen assembled on its floor. It was on this floor that the first ever £1,000,000 cheque was signed. The social amenities provided by the Exchange were situated behind the beautiful panelling on the balcony.*

*The Pier Head Building in 1923, the year after the Great Western Railway took control of the docks. The West Dock still appears busy, but elsewhere in the port the Depression was beginning to bite.*

recovered to fight its way through the Depression and remained the most important of the Cardiff shipowners for many years to come.

After the war, many shipowners, some of them newcomers, anticipated a return to pre-war conditions and there was a short-lived artificial surge in trade. In a spirit of optimism, orders for new vessels were placed and a record 122 companies were registered at Cardiff in 1919. It was not long before the demand for Welsh coal receded as the Great Depression of the interwar years began. Cardiff now paid the price of relying on this one commodity for its prosperity. In the 1930s only five million tons of coal, half the amount shipped in 1914, were exported from the docks and unemployment among dockers rose to nearly 50 percent.

By 1921 the Cardiff fleet was worth only 20 percent of its value a year earlier. Some of the docksmen foresaw the false dawn but others faced ruin. Small investors went bankrupt or ended up in gaol for fraud. The collapse of Sven Hansen's business empire was perhaps the most spectacular as the Depression began to bite. Hansen was a leading light in Cardiff's social circle and was knighted for his wartime services. In 1918 he owned 12 large steamers and a colliery, but he overstretched himself when he speculated in new ships. He also invested in a yard for building and repairing ships at Bideford, and, when the crash came, he was forced to sell everything at knock-down prices.

Lord Glanely was probably the most far-sighted of the docksmen. Anticipating that the post-war boom in shipping was only temporary, he sold all his vessels that had survived the war in 1919. He then re-ordered fewer ships suited to the post-war economic climate, and even during the most difficult years of the Depression his company was one of the few able to pay a dividend to its shareholders.

*Lord Glanely leading in Singapore, winner of the St Leger in 1930. Having made his fortune at the docks, Glanely found another profitable venture when he became a leading racehorse owner after World War One.*

Glanely became a JP and Deputy Lord Lieutenant for Glamorgan and, for a time, lived at The Court in St Fagans. He had a passion for horses before the war and now became one of the most renowned racehorse owners in the country. In 1919 his horse, Dominion, was the favourite for the Derby and was widely backed by people in Cardiff. Lord Glanely won the Derby but not with the favourite. It was his other horse, Grand Parade, an outsider at 33–1, who came in the winner. Glanely was certainly not the most popular man in Cardiff for some time after that. Over the next few years his horses won all five classic races, and he invested in 3,500 acres of land at Newmarket, where he had his own stables and a stud farm. During World War Two Glanely retired to Weston and suffered a tragic end to his life when he was killed in an air raid in 1942.

In World War Two Cardiff Docks played a major role in Britain's history for the last time. Vital supplies from North America were unloaded at the port and, when the United States entered the war, 75 percent of its requirements were shipped through the docks of South Wales. From 1943 onwards US forces sailed directly into Cardiff in preparation for the D-Day landings. Despite this activity, the docksmen, governed by strict controls, did not make the handsome profits they had during World War One.

*The bust of Lord Glanely stands near that of Sir William Reardon-Smith in the Marble Hall. It is a recognition of his charitable work and his role in public life, particularly as President of University College.*

After the war, exports of coal from Cardiff once more declined and eventually stopped altogether in 1958. One by one the great shipping firms ceased to exist, and the few companies now operating at Cardiff bear no resemblance to the great names of the past. In 1966 John Cory & Co ceased to be shipowners and now operate from Capital Towers as shipping agents. Their splendid offices in Butetown are just another monument to an historic past. Cory Brothers are now freight agents, with their business based in Newport. Evan Thomas and Radcliffe, after sustaining heavy losses in World War Two, gave up their shipping operations in 1983. The Reardon-Smith Line, by trading

worldwide and investing in modern ships, had successfully ridden out the Depression. However, the decline of the British merchant fleet after World War Two led to huge losses, and in 1985 the company was forced to close.

The once thriving docks are now a mere shadow of their former selves. The West Dock, the forerunner of the others, was filled in more than 40 years ago. The former East Dock provides an attractive setting for the County Hall but is now an enclosed stretch of water. The Roath Basin is sometimes used for ships visiting Cardiff, but only the Queen Alexandra and, to a lesser extent, the Roath Dock are still in use for what was once the greatest coal-exporting port in the world.

At the Exchange, the bell signifying the start of business rang for the last time early in 1961. The building might have provided a home for the Welsh Assembly when proposals for devolution were first put to the Welsh people in 1979. At that time they overwhelmingly rejected the idea. The Coal Exchange is now run by the Macob Group, and the floor, which was so busy a century ago, is now used for conferences, public meetings and concerts.

In the 1970s large areas of Cardiff Bay were a miserable scene of dereliction. Then, in the following decade, work began to transform the district into the pleasant environment it now offers. With its new housing, restaurants and shops,

*The unusual pagoda-type design of Cardiff's County Hall is an unmistakeable landmark alongside the old East Dock. When it opened in 1988, it marked the beginning of the revival of Cardiff Bay.*

*The once thriving commercial life of the docks lies in the past, but Cardiff Bay is now one of the city's major tourist attractions. Past and present combine as the Pier Head Building stands tall amid the well-designed modern development of Mermaid Quay.*

the bay has become popular with both tourists and the people of Cardiff. Only the ghosts remain of those halcyon days before 1914 when coal and shipping created the city of Cardiff as we know it today.

**Further reading:**
**Jenkins, J.G. & D.** *Cardiff Shipowners*, National Museum of Wales, 1986.
**Evans, C., S. Dodsworth & J. Barnett**, *Below the Bridge*, National Museum of Wales, 1984.

*Chapter 3*
# Cardiff's Tribute to Scott of the Antarctic

One of the most notable features at Roath Park is the Clock Tower resembling a lighthouse at the southern end of the lake. The dedication above its door reads 'To the memory of Captain R.F. Scott… and his faithful companions… who sailed in the S.S. *Terra Nova* from the port of Cardiff June 15th 1910 to locate the South Pole, and, in pursuit of that great and successful scientific task, laid down their lives in the Antarctic Regions. March 1912. BRITONS ALL AND VERY GALLANT GENTLEMEN'.

It might seem strange that Robert Falcon Scott should decide to set out from Cardiff in his attempt to be the first man to reach the South Pole. The reason lies in the generous contributions made to the expedition from the shipowners of the port. The Welsh connection originally stemmed from Lieutenant Teddy Evans, whose grandfather was a Cardiff man. In 1909 Evans had drawn up plans for an expedition to the South Pole, and W.E. Davies, the editor of the *Western Mail*, suggested that the venture might receive substantial support from Welsh businessmen if it could be linked to Cardiff. Soon afterwards Evans met Captain Scott, who was in the process of planning his own voyage, and the two men agreed to work together, with Scott in command and Evans as his first lieutenant. It was Evans who suggested that Cardiff could play an important role in financing the British Antarctic expedition, and though Scott had serious doubts about the optimism engendered by the editor of the *Western Mail* he agreed that his lieutenant should go to Cardiff in an effort to raise funds towards the £50,000 the venture would need.

Strongly supported by the *Western Mail*, Evans came to Cardiff in October 1909 in his search for financial backing. He aimed his appeal towards the wealthy

*The elegant Clock Tower, overlooking the lake at Roath Park, is one of Cardiff's most notable monuments. Completed in 1915 at a cost of £159, it was officially unveiled by its donor, C.T. Bowring, in October 1918.*

docksmen and stressed the advantages which publicity and sponsorship could bring to Cardiff. Evans soon found an enthusiastic ally in Daniel Radcliffe, one of the largest shipowners in the city.

Scott did not find it easy, either in Britain or in the Empire, to raise the capital he required for his ambition. His attempts to arouse interest were often met with scepticism, and only the business community of Cardiff, especially the docksmen, seemed to have any real enthusiasm for the enterprise. Indeed, the expedition might well have foundered but for the influence of W.E. Davies. He drew on his friendship with David Lloyd George, the Chancellor of the Exchequer, and persuaded him to make a government grant of £20,000 towards the expedition.

Eventually £2,500 was raised in Cardiff, £500 more than any other city or town in Britain. Apart from the cash donations, the docksmen provided at least another £5,000 in resources and equipment for the journey. The coal bunkers of the *Terra Nova* were filled free of charge in Cardiff, the largest contribution coming from the Crown Patent Fuel Company. Technical assistance and cooking utensils were also forthcoming from Welsh companies.

*This souvenir card, showing the* Terra Nova *departing from Cardiff, reflects the pride felt in the city as Captain Scott and Lieutenant Evans set forth on their historic but ill-fated voyage.*

The Dash for the South Pole.
The "Terra Nova" R.Y.S. leaving Cardiff, June 15th, 1910.

The Channel Dry Dock agreed to paint the ship in readiness for its journey and repaired several leaks in its hull. Scott had been forced to register the ship as a yacht in order to avoid the regulations of the Board of Trade relating to crew's living quarters and, much more seriously, the danger of overloading. Even so, when it set out to sea, *Terra Nova* was considerably overloaded with equipment.

Strangely, few of the studies of Scott's expedition have paid tribute to the vital role the city played in financing the voyage, but, in return for such generous assistance, Scott was more than happy to begin his journey to the Antarctic from Cardiff. On 10 June 1910 the *Terra Nova* weighed anchor at the Roath Dock, and when Scott came ashore he spoke of Cardiff's enthusiastic support 'which, if equalled, has not been excelled by any other port'.

For the next few days Cardiff opened its heart to the crew of the *Terra Nova*. Lieutenant Evans and Kathleen Scott stayed at the Mansion House as guests of the Lord Mayor, and on Sunday 12 June Scott returned from London to join them.

That same day the ship was opened to visitors but, with an admission charge of 2s 6d, only about 100 people took advantage of this offer.

The Chamber of Commerce invited the officers and crew to a farewell dinner on 13 June, though the separate venues indicate the class distinction of the times. The officers dined at the Alexander Room in the Royal Hotel, where the 7s 6d menu included such delicacies as fillet of beef *Terra Nova* and South Pole iced pudding. Background music was provided by a string orchestra and among the items in their repertoire was a piece entitled *Hero of the South*. Meanwhile, just a short distance away, the other members of the crew were dining from the 2s 6d menu at Barry's Restaurant. Later in the evening the two groups came together in the Royal Hotel for a smoking concert, where they mingled with the civic dignitaries and the docksmen who had given their help so generously.

Naturally, presentations and speeches marked the occasion. A flag bearing the arms of Cardiff was presented by the Lord Mayor, John Chappell. In his response Scott promised that it would be flying as the *Terra Nova* left Cardiff and again when they reached the South Pole. It was rumoured that several among the audience neither knew what the Pole was nor where it was to be found. One councillor suggested the flag ought to be nailed to the South Pole, while a

*Terra Nova on 11 June 1910. It is loading 100 tons of steam coal for its journey. The previous day the ship had taken on another 300 tons of fuel. All these supplies were a gift to the expedition by local companies.*

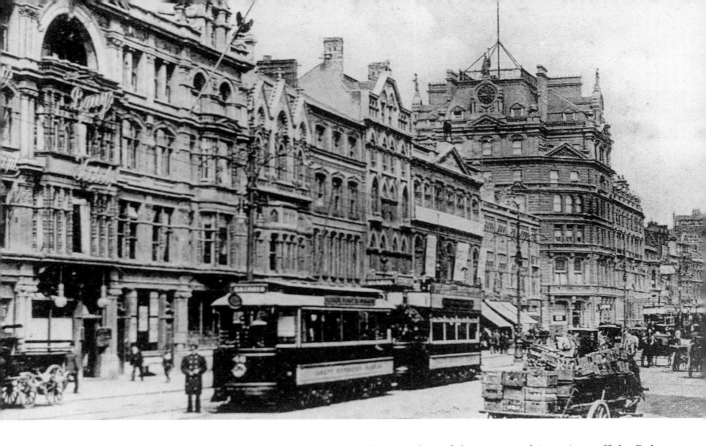

*Barry's Hotel in the early 20th century. Scott's crew enjoyed a convivial evening at this popular restaurant before joining the officers at the Royal Hotel, on the right of the photograph, later in the evening.*

docksman surreptitiously asked a member of the crew to chip a piece off the Pole and smuggle it back for his private collection. Much more importantly from Scott's point of view, Radcliffe and other docksmen contributed a further £1,000 towards the cost of the expedition, 'amid a scene of great enthusiasm'. This final donation saved Scott from the possible embarrassment of having insufficient funds to pay the wages of his crew.

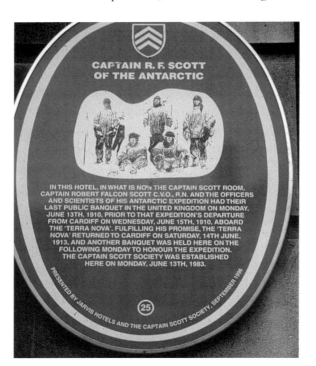

CAPTAIN R. F. SCOTT OF THE ANTARCTIC

IN THIS HOTEL, IN WHAT IS NOW THE CAPTAIN SCOTT ROOM, CAPTAIN ROBERT FALCON SCOTT C.V.O., R.N. AND THE OFFICERS AND SCIENTISTS OF HIS ANTARCTIC EXPEDITION HAD THEIR LAST PUBLIC BANQUET IN THE UNITED KINGDOM ON MONDAY, JUNE 13TH, 1910, PRIOR TO THAT EXPEDITION'S DEPARTURE FROM CARDIFF ON WEDNESDAY, JUNE 15TH, 1910, ABOARD THE 'TERRA NOVA'. FULFILLING HIS PROMISE, THE 'TERRA NOVA' RETURNED TO CARDIFF ON SATURDAY, 14TH JUNE, 1913, AND ANOTHER BANQUET WAS HELD HERE ON THE FOLLOWING MONDAY TO HONOUR THE EXPEDITION. THE CAPTAIN SCOTT SOCIETY WAS ESTABLISHED HERE ON MONDAY, JUNE 13TH, 1983.

PRESENTED BY JARVIS HOTELS AND THE CAPTAIN SCOTT SOCIETY, SEPTEMBER 1996

(25)

*This plaque at the Royal Hotel was donated by the Captain Scott Society and Jarvis Hotels in 1996 to commemorate the banquet held there on 13 June 1910. At present the plaque is missing while the hotel completes its refurbishment.*

As Scott and Evans conducted their round of social engagements, Scott promised that Cardiff would be the port to which the *Terra Nova* would return after its long voyage. On their final evening in Cardiff a civic reception for more than 800 guests was held at the City Hall. The Lord Mayor once more

offered his good wishes to Scott and his crew and rather presumptuously commented, 'never has Cardiff played its part more thoroughly as the capital of the Principality'. It would be another 45 years before Cardiff had that honour.

*At the Mansion House on 14 June, Scott was entertained by the Lord Mayor, John Chappell. From left to right: Captain Scott, John Chappell, Lieutenant Evans, Mrs Scott, Mrs Chappell, Mrs Evans.*

*On 15 June 1910* Terra Nova *set forth from the Roath Dock to begin its long voyage. A pleasure craft follows at a safe distance as young and old jostle to have a better view.*

*The paddle steamer* Devonia *is among the accompanying vessels. On board are many of Cardiff's leading citizens, enjoying the carnival atmosphere as the band plays an accompaniment of patriotic airs.*

Next day, Wednesday 15 June, the *Terra Nova* departed from the Roath Dock at one o'clock. Among the special guests on board were the Lord Mayor and Daniel Radcliffe, who had done so much to make the journey possible. A huge crowd gathered along the shore to cheer the vessel as it slowly made its way out to sea. A flotilla of small craft and pleasure steamers, full of well-wishers, followed in its wake and among them, on board the *Devonia*, were members of the Chamber

*Scott, Evans and Jenkins, the pilot, on the bridge of* Terra Nova. *Later in the day, Scott returned to Cardiff with the Lord Mayor before leaving for London. Still hoping to drum up financial support, he did not rejoin his ship until it reached Simonstown in South Africa.*

of Commerce and city councillors. The screaming of sirens, the piercing shrieks of steam whistles, the beeping of hooters and the booming of cannon all contributed to a deafening farewell. Streamers and bunting, trailing from warehouses and offices, heightened the carnival atmosphere. As the *Terra Nova* prepared to sail under its own steam, a couple of leeks were hoisted alongside the Welsh flag, a gesture which brought huge cheers from the accompanying vessels. As Scott left the vessel and returned to Cardiff with the Lord Mayor, he turned to Radcliffe and uttered what might be considered prophetic words: 'I will reach the South Pole or I will never come back again'.

Thus the *Terra Nova* set out on its historic journey and the rest of the story is well known. Despite the emphasis on the scientific nature of the expedition, Scott hoped to be the first man to reach the South Pole. The Norwegian explorer, Roald Amundsen, courteously informed him that it was also his intention to strive for this objective. On 4 January 1912 Scott set out on the last 150 miles to the Pole with four companions, while the principal support party returned to their main base at Cape Evans. As the Antarctic winter closed in, Teddy Evans returned to Cardiff, where he renewed old friendships with Radcliffe and other supporters of the expedition.

Just over a year after Evans had bade his commander farewell, he returned to Antarctica, where he first heard of the the fate that had befallen Scott and his companions. They had reached the Pole on 17 January 1912, only to find the

*As* Terra Nova *rounds Penarth Head, it begins to lose most of its well-wishers. Ahead lies the long, arduous journey to the Antarctic, and in Australia Scott will learn that Amundsen is also planning to reach the South Pole.*

Norwegian flag fluttering in the breeze. Amundsen had won the race by 34 days. The disappointment must have been intense, and on the return journey of 900 miles the small contingent met with tragedy. The weather was atrocious, and though supply dumps had been laid along their route the nearest one to safety, known as One-ton Depot, proved to be just out of reach in those dreadful conditions. Petty officer Edgar Evans from Swansea was the first to die. Captain Lawrence Oates, crippled from frostbite and slowing the others down, bravely sacrificed himself in a blizzard. His death was in vain as Scott, Dr Wilson and Lieutenant Bowers all perished in March amid the icy wastes of Antarctica. Their bodies were found eight months later and a cairn was erected on the rim of the Great Ice Barrier with the epitaph 'To strive, to seek, to find, and not to yield'.

When the news was cabled back to Britain in February 1913, a painting of the *Terra Nova* was draped in black at the Coal Exchange and a memorial service was held in St John's Church. A few months later, on 14 June, *Terra Nova* once more berthed at the East Dock, almost three years to the day since leaving Cardiff.

From its foremast flew the Welsh Dragon and the city's coat of arms. At the request of Kathleen Scott, now Lady Scott, an honour personally conferred by the King, the initial welcome was private. She was accompanied aboard by a few

*Though the expedition had ended in tragedy, large crowds greeted* Terra Nova *when it returned to Cardiff in 1913 as Scott had promised. The photograph shows Lady Scott leaving the ship after a private welcome.*

friends and her son, Peter. Later they were joined by Daniel Radcliffe and others who had supported the expedition. Thousands of people congregated on the cliffs of Penarth and around the harbour, and as little Peter wandered around the ship Commander Evans handed him his cap to acknowledge the crowds cheering from the shore.

Special trains brought more than 60,000 spectators to view the ship over the next few weeks. At a dinner, held once again in the Royal Hotel, the two flags, bearing Cardiff's coat of arms and the Welsh Dragon, were handed back to the Lord Mayor. In his speech, Evans said it was fitting that *Terra Nova* had come back to the port 'because it was Cardiff that had made the expedition possible'.

Scott's lieutenant went on to become Lord Mountevans, and in World War One he commanded the *Broke,* a destroyer which earned fame when it rammed a German ship. As German sailors leapt on to his ship, probably seeking safety, Evans gave orders to repel boarders. From that time forth he was known as 'Evans of the *Broke*'. The *Terra Nova* was sold back to her original owners, Bowring Brothers, to resume whaling duties off the coast of Newfoundland. The ship itself was lost in 1943 when it struck an iceberg off the coast of Greenland.

When news of the deaths of Scott and his companions reached Cardiff, an appeal committee was set up to erect a memorial to these gallant men. The response to these efforts was disappointing and only £430 was collected. The money was partly used to donate a *Terra Nova* bed at the Royal Hamadryad

ROBERT FALCON SCOTT K.C.B. C.V.O.
BORN 6 JUNE 1868 AT DEVONPORT, DIED 29TH MARCH 1912
WHILST RETVRNING FROM THE SOVTH POLE
CAPTAIN IN HIS MAJESTY'S ROYAL NAVY, ANTARCTIC EXPLORER
COMMANDER OF THE BRITISH ANTARCTIC EXPEDITION 1910
LEFT CARDIFF IN THE "TERRA NOVA" ON THE 15TH JVNE 1910,
REACHED THE SOVTH POLE 18TH JANVARY 1912.
"TO STRIVE, TO SEEK, TO FIND, AND NOT TO YIELD."
VICTORY FOR HIM WAS SWALLOWED VP IN DEATH
THIS TABLET
WAS ERECTED TO COMMEMORATE THE MEMORY OF ONE
WHO SACRIFICED HIS LIFE TO OBTAIN GLORY FOR HIS BELOVED COVNTRY

ALDERMAN MORGAN THOMAS JP.          DAN RADCLIFFE JP.          J. L. WHEATLEY
LORD MAYOR 1912-13                  HON. TREASVRER              TOWN CLERK

*This monument in Cardiff Bay, somewhat ironically near the Norwegian Church, is a more recent addition to the story of Scott and Cardiff. It was unveiled by the Princess Royal on 6 June 2003.*

Hospital, while the remainder was spent on a plaque which can still be seen on the main staircase of the City Hall.

It was left to F.C. Bowring, the prospective Liberal Parliamentary candidate for Cardiff, to ensure that Scott's connection with the city would not be forgotten. Initially he suggested that the figurehead of the *Terra Nova* should be displayed at Roath Park. When the unveiling of the figurehead took place in December 1913, Bowring pointed out that it would soon rot if left exposed to the elements and later it was presented to the National Museum of Wales.

As an alternative, Bowring announced that he was prepared to provide the

Opposite page: *This plaque is one of the many tributes to Captain Scott in Cardiff. It is the work of W.W. Wagstaff and can be seen on the left-hand staircase inside the City Hall.*

*The Captain Scott Society met regularly in this room at the Royal Hotel until it was closed for the hotel's renovation. The display cases contain memorabilia of the Antarctic expedition.*

money to build the Clock Tower at Roath Park with a model of the *Terra Nova* at its summit. More recently a mosaic statue, paying tribute to everyone involved in the Antarctic expedition, has been erected in Cardiff Bay, looking out over the waters from which the ship had sailed nearly a century before.

The Captain Scott Society in Cardiff was founded in 1983, with Sir Peter Scott as its first president. The members of the society met annually on 13 June to re-enact that farewell dinner of 1910 in the Captain Scott Room. Recently the hotel has been closed for refurbishment, but now it is open again it is likely that this tradition will once more be renewed.

Much has been written about Scott's planning of the Antarctic expedition and whether he was mistaken in using horses to pull his sledges, rather than dogs as Amundsen had done. Yet on that June day in 1910, as the *Terra Nova* sailed from Cardiff, few people doubted that they were witnessing the beginning of a great adventure. Whatever mistakes he made, Captain Scott and his faithful companions are deservedly remembered among the great heroes of British exploration, and the lighthouse in Roath Park is a permanent tribute to their courage.

**Further Reading:**
**Johnson A.M.** *Scott of the Antarctic and Cardiff*, University College, Cardiff, 1984.

## Chapter 4
# The Friend of Freedom

As shoppers and tourists pause for a cup of tea or a sandwich at the snack bar on Hayes Island, few of them are aware of the discord once created by the nearby statue of John Batchelor. He had been a controversial figure throughout his lifetime and, when the monument was first erected, it aroused passionate feelings.

Batchelor was born in Newport in 1820, and, after working in the shipbuilding industry in Scotland and America, he came to Cardiff in 1843. He and his brother,

*Though moved a few yards occasionally, the statue of John Batchelor still remains in the vicinity of Hayes Island. It has survived assaults, ranging from daubed paint to traffic cones and beer bottles, for more than 120 years.*

*The old course of the Taff as it flowed to the west of St Mary Street. Batchelors' first yard can be seen in the foreground. Later the Central Hotel, recently destroyed by fire, occupied the site.*

*The Congregational Church in Charles Street was John Batchelor's place of worship. Ebenezer, as it is now called, is a striking example of the unusual use of ballast materials brought from every corner of the world.*

Sidney, bought a small shipyard and timber business at the southern end of St Mary Street, not far from where the Great Western Hotel stands today. The diversion of the Taff, when the South Wales Railway was built, forced the Batchelors to look for new premises. They moved to a new site at the head of the West Dock, but the second Marquess of Bute refused to give the brothers a long-term lease on the land. Instead, he only allowed them to rent the land on an annual basis, a decision John believed was a response to his political views. He had already shown his radical leanings with his sympathy towards the Chartist movement, and in 1846 he attacked the Corn Laws, which deprived the poor of cheap bread.

Batchelor was a staunch Congregationalist, and in 1848 he came into conflict with the Anglican Church when he refused to pay the church rate. One of his timber wagons was seized towards payment, but he was able to buy it back for the paltry sum of 12s. He made his Nonconformist views even more apparent in 1862 when he was a delegate at the Liberation Society, formed to separate religion from state patronage. He argued that 'Christianity should be supported not by compulsory enactments, forced exactions and state endowments, but by the voluntary zeal and liberality of its friends'. In later years he played a leading role in the building of the Congregational Church in Charles Street where he worshipped.

For a time the displeasure of the Bute family did little to hamper the prosperity of Batchelor Brothers. They built and repaired ships and had a profitable timber business, to which they added by purchasing timber yards at Merthyr and Aberdare. One of the earliest ships launched from their yard was the *Taff*, a sailing vessel that carried passengers to New York.

After the death of his first wife Hannah Batchelor married Fanny Burder from Essex in 1851, and the census that year reveals that they lived in a fine house next door to his brother in Charles Street. John was described as a timber merchant, employing 40 men, with additional income from land and mortgages. Over the next few years his family grew considerably and Fanny bore him 10 children to add to the two daughters he had by his first marriage. Later they moved to Cliff Villa, overlooking the Bristol Channel at Penarth.

It was when Batchelor became involved in local politics as a Liberal that his feud with the Bute Estate intensified. Prior to his death in 1848, the second Marquess had dominated the town's affairs, and few people in Cardiff dared to oppose his wishes. For the next 20 years, until his son came of age, trustees handled the estate. It was during this period that the Liberal and Nonconformist element in the town grew in strength, and it was John Batchelor, 'the friend of freedom', as his statue proclaims, who led the battle against the 'Castle Party'.

Elected as a street commissioner in 1848, Batchelor proposed a proper sewerage system for Cardiff but this was rejected as too expensive. He then played a leading

*Charles Street was still a residential area at the beginning of the 20th century. In 1851, when Batchelor lived at number 10, the road was described as 'one of the most fashionable streets in the town'.*

*Leading off Queen Street, Mason's Arms Court was among the most notorious slums of Cardiff in the 19th century. It was against conditions like this that Batchelor campaigned and often aroused hostility.*

role in petitioning for the implementation of the Public Health Act, which would allow the Cardiff Corporation to improve sanitation and living conditions in the town. Much of the cost for doing this would fall on the Bute family, and not surprisingly their agent, Edward Priest Richards, attacked 'that most dangerous and insidious of centralizing schemes, the Public Health Act'. The petition was successful and an investigation revealed the appalling living conditions in Cardiff at that time. The application of the Public Health Act followed, and Batchelor's part in bringing about benefits in public health made him a leading political figure in Cardiff. He became a Liberal councillor in 1850 and three years later was mayor of the town.

Already regarded by the Bute trustees as a dangerous radical, John Batchelor attracted their wrath again in the General Election of 1852. The trustees nominated John Nicholl as the Tory candidate. They were confident of success as no one had ever dared to oppose a Bute nomination. Batchelor took a prominent role in persuading his friend, Walter Coffin, to stand as the Liberal candidate. In a close contest Coffin was elected, and Cardiff became a Liberal stronghold for the next 40 years. The result aroused the anger of the Marchioness of Bute and the trustees in no uncertain terms, and Cooper's Fields, where the Militia band played on Sunday afternoons, was closed for a time. Later the gates were re-opened but Coffin's supporters were forbidden entry. When Mrs Batchelor entered Cooper's Fields with friends, who were not on the black list, she was ordered to leave.

Much more serious was the harassment Batchelor's business faced from the trustees. In 1854 one of his ships, carrying a load of timber, was refused access to the West Dock on the grounds that it was too large. As a result, it was diverted to Bristol and the opportunity for a return cargo was lost. Batchelor also claimed that the trustees were denying him proper facilities for his business. Consequently timber cargoes had to be towed out of the dock to the timber yard, resulting in considerable loss and damage. Eventually a compromise was reached, and Batchelor Brothers were given the use of cranes and storage facilities.

In 1857 the Batchelors were forced to quit their timber yard and moved to a new site in Stuart Street, where they established a ship-building and repair

business at the Penarth Roads Graving Dock. Once again John complained he was being persecuted when the trustees leased a plot of land in a position that silted up the entrance to the graving dock. On this occasion the trustees were forced to back down and a court order compelled them to remove all obstructions at their own expense. Despite their problems, Batchelor Brothers built more than 10 vessels between 1859 and 1870, among them fine clipper ships such as the *James Marychurch* and the *Ella Nicol*.

It is not surprising, in view of his quarrels with the Bute Estate, that Batchelor was a leading figure in the formation of the Penarth Dock and Railway Company, which opened in 1865. The Butes opposed this threat to their monopoly, and L.V. Shirley, agent to the Bute family, later claimed Batchelor's action showed he had little love for his adopted town, since Penarth Dock took trade away from Cardiff.

The commercial panic of 1866 resulted in heavy losses for the Batchelors, especially when some of their contractors went out of business. In March 1872 John revealed the extent of the firm's problems when he wrote to his son, Herbert, pointing out the difficulties he was experiencing in paying his employees. Facing ruin, Batchelor retired from the world of commerce. His friends in the Liberal Party did not forget him, and they set up a fund on his behalf, which eventually raised the considerable sum of £5,000.

*This engraving of 1859 shows a busy scene at the ship-building yard of Batchelor Brothers. It was their third and final yard, and, though they built several fine ships, their business collapsed in 1872.*

*The* Ella Nichol, *launched in 1872, was the last ship to be built at Batchelors' yard. It was ordered by Edward Nicholl and was still in use as late as 1921.*

Nor did John give up public life. He was unanimously elected President of the Cardiff Liberal Association, and, after the Education Act of 1870, he accepted the chairmanship of the school boards at Cardiff and Penarth. He also became Inspector of Coal to the Crown Agents of the Colonies, a post which brought him a salary of £600 a year. Once again his enemies accused him of 'political jobbery'.

John Batchelor died at Penarth in May 1883 after suffering from a brain tumour. The funeral service took place at his church in Charles Street, where the minister spoke of his 'unselfish devotion to what he conceived to be a righteous cause'. There were also tributes from the local Liberal MP, Edward Reed, and the Prime Minister, William Gladstone. As the funeral cortège made its way to Cathays Cemetery, thousands lined the route, led by the Mayor.

Three years later, Batchelor's statue was unveiled on 16 October 1886. Cast in bronze, it was erected on Hayes Island. At a time when party politics were bitterly fought in

*This is one of the few surviving portraits of John Batchelor, taken late in his life. Perhaps worn out by his battles with the Bute Estate, he died at the relatively early age of 63.*

Cardiff, Batchelor had been a man who aroused passionate feelings. The vicar of St John's, who spoke at his funeral, said 'he was a strong man and like all strong men he made enemies'. Batchelor's allegations that the Butes had waged a vindictive campaign against him had some substance, though even his friends were prepared to admit that John was a sensitive man who took offence very easily. He was certainly a fiery debater, and in the 1881 local elections he had a bitter dispute with L.V. Shirley in which both men hurled harsh diatribes at one another. So it is not surprising that while the statue was received by the Liberals with satisfaction it aroused fury among Batchelor's political opponents.

A correspondent, naming himself 'Admirer of High Art', called it a 'hideous effigy', portraying Batchelor, 'the old election hand', in a pair of oilskin leggings several sizes too large for him. These remarks were trivial compared with a letter published in the *Western Mail*. It was sent by a local solicitor, Thomas Ensor, who suggested a suitable epitaph for the statue. It contained such vitriolic phrases as 'A traitor to the Crown, a reviler of the aristocracy, a hater of the clergy... sincerely mourned by unpaid creditors to the amount of £50,000... who, at the close of a wasted and mis-spent life, died a demagogue and a pauper'. Lascelles Carr, the editor of the *Western Mail*, soon encountered the reaction of Batchelor's family when two of John's sons waylaid him outside the railway station and attacked him with a whip. Cyril and Llewellyn Batchelor were fined 1s for this assault by a sympathetic Stipendiary Magistrate who said they had acted under provocation.

*Lascelles Carr, the controversial editor of the* Western Mail. *He published Ensor's letter with its bitter attack on Batchelor's statue. Though the* Western Mail *was a Tory newspaper, Carr himself was a radical Conservative and in 1873 organised a public fund on behalf of striking miners.*

Batchelor's friends decided to sue Ensor on the grounds of criminal libel, and in February 1887 the case was presented at the Nisi Prius Court in Cardiff. Counsel for the plaintiffs claimed that libel against a dead person was indictable if it might lead to a breach of the peace. The defence argued that the law of libel did not apply to a dead man. The judge, Sir James Stephen, agreed with their interpretation of the law and directed the jury to acquit on the grounds that 'the dead have no rights and can suffer no wrongs'. At the same time he indicated that if John Batchelor were still alive the words would be libellous. The verdict did not please the Liberal *Cardiff Times,* which stated bitterly 'We wonder what the learned judge would think if someone proclaimed that his father was a liar and a thief'. However, there was no appeal and the case, which attracted national interest, created a precedent for similar cases in the future.

The statue continued to cause friction. A petition signed by 1,200 people demanded its removal. 'A court packed with Radical magistrates', as the *Western Mail* contemptuously called it, fined William Thorne £15 for throwing eggs, paint and tar at the statue the day after the libel case. In June 1887 a special meeting of the council met to discuss the Town Clerk's proposal that the statue should be removed, as it was occupying land worth more than £10,000, and was erected to a man 'associated with one political party'. The debate was enlivened by boos and hisses from the gallery, but no action was taken.

Between 1908–10, when the Cardiff Tramways Parcels Office was built, there were proposals to remove the statue to Cathays Park. Imagine the irony if it had been placed near the statue of the third Marquess of Bute! As it is, the monument to the man who attracted so much controversy in his lifetime, and after his death, has been moved only a few yards away from its original position and remains a part of Hayes Island.

**Further reading:**

**Batchelor, K.B.** *John Batchelor*, Holt Magazine, Holt, 1975 (Cardiff Central Library).

**Williams, S. (Ed.)** *The Cardiff Book*, Vol.3, Stewart Williams, 1977.

*Sir James Fitzjames Stephens, who presided over the famous libel case. His belief that there could be free criticism of the dead was unpopular with Batchelor's friends, but it became a part of English law.*

*This view of Hayes Island was taken in 1905 and shows the original position of Batchelor's statue. At that time the tall trees of today were mere saplings and the Central Library was only 20 years old.*

# Chapter 5
# The Humble Dwellings
# that won an Award

Spectators flocking to the Millennium Stadium for a big match often take a short cut along Womanby Street. Few of them notice what lies behind the iron railings near its junction with Quay Street. Yet here lies Jones Court, one of the most interesting reminders of 19th-century Cardiff. A plaque at its entrance tells us that Jones Court was originally built by the second Marquess of Bute to provide homes for Irish immigrants. The Marquess brought them to Cardiff to build the West Dock because his Welsh workers were striking for better pay and conditions. He chose to break the strike rather than yield to their demands.

*The plaque at Jones Court was placed there when the site was restored in the 1980s. The houses were the last example of working-class accommodation from the Victorian period.*

JONES COURT

THE NEW BUILDING TO THE EAST STANDS WHERE TRACES OF OCCUPATION OF THE SITE FROM THE 12TH UNTIL THE LATE 17TH CENTURY HAVE BEEN FOUND, THE TERRACE OF COTTAGES WAS BUILT IN THE 1830'S TO HOUSE LABOURERS IMPORTED BY THE MARQUIS OF BUTE FOR CONSTRUCTION OF THE DOCKS AND HAVE NOW BEEN RENOVATED AS OFFICE ACCOMMODATION TO FORM PART OF THIS DEVELOPMENT

CARDIFF CITY COUNCIL ACQUIRED THE WHOLE SITE AT THE TURN OF THE 20TH CENTURY AND THE NEW BUILDINGS TO THE SOUTH AND WEST OF THE COURT OCCUPY THE FORMER SITE OF THE CITY'S WEIGHTS & MEASURES BUILDING

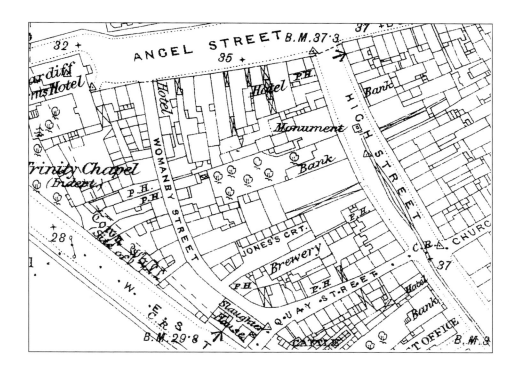

*This map was a survey of the district around Jones Court in 1876. Within a few years the slaughter house and the cattle market were moved elsewhere. Angel Street became Castle Street and the Cardiff Arms Hotel was demolished to widen the road after the Cardiff Improvement Act of 1875.*

The site of Jones Court is ancient, and an archaeological survey a few years ago revealed traces of mediaeval walls and dwellings, dating as far back as the 12th century. The court was built in the late 1830s, just as Cardiff was entering into a period of remarkable growth. Its population was approaching 10,000 and expanding rapidly every year. Families from every corner of Britain were arriving in the town, seeking work at the docks or on the railways, and housing of any kind was at a premium. The 10 houses in Jones Court cost just over £100 each to build and, while the rent was only a few shillings a week, the living conditions, especially for the earliest residents, were primitive.

In 1850 a report by the Board of Health inspector, T.W. Rammell, drew attention to the appalling sanitation and living conditions of the thickly-crowded courts in the heart of Cardiff. In Jones Court the houses were back to back and each dwelling consisted of two rooms, one up and one down, so that both light and air were extremely restricted. The court had no paving and, because the front door was not raised above street level, surface water was inclined to flow into the houses. Drainage was virtually non-existent, and as toilet facilities were woefully inadequate the tendency was to empty what was politely called 'night soil' on to the old Town Quay. This was no more than 50 metres from Jones Court and there the disgusting deposits lay until the high tide washed them away.

The houses at Jones Court did not have their own supply of drinking water, and the nearest public pump, often dry during the summer, was 200 metres away in St Mary Street. For other purposes, such as washing or cleaning, water was drawn

from the polluted waters of the Taff. In 1849 a cholera epidemic was raging throughout Cardiff, and the death toll was at its worst in these over-populated courts and alleys. Nearly 400 people died from cholera or diarrhoea during the year, and Rammell describes it as 'a fearful visitation for a population not exceeding 12,000'. In Jones Court and its surrounding streets alone, these diseases had claimed nine victims.

In Womanby Street the stench from the slaughter house was so abominable that residents were forced to keep their windows and doors closed. One butcher refused to use the place because of the drunkenness, fighting and stealing, which were daily occurrences. Recently there had been two deaths from cholera in a dwelling near the slaughter house, and among Rammell's recommendations was a suggestion that the building should be moved well away from people's homes. Even so, it remained in use until 1877, despite complaints about the danger to public health and the continual lowing of cattle, which kept everyone awake at night.

Who was living in Jones Court when Rammell was writing his report? The census of 1851 shows that the 10 houses were occupied by 45 people. They had come to Cardiff from various parts of Britain but the majority were of West Country origin. Strangely enough, no one from Ireland was living there, so presumably the dock workers of the 1830s had moved elsewhere. Most of the inhabitants, as might be expected, were labourers, but John Cornish from Bideford was a leather worker and John Morrish from Gloucester described himself as a maltster. Rather surprisingly, we find that Elizabeth Rees, a widow of 70 who lived at 3 Jones Court, could afford to hire a maidservant. Perhaps her three children, all of whom were working, paid for this luxury, though it is likely that the servant's reward for her toil was little more than food and lodgings. The most over-crowded house was at number eight, where James Williams lived with his wife,

*This photograph of Womanby Street in the 1880s may have been taken from the entrance to Jones Court. Next door to the Horse and Groom is the Independent Congregational Chapel. Overlooking the street is the Clock Tower of the castle.*

*Jones Court was still inhabited in 1892 when this picture was taken. A few years later the dwellings were vacated and the site was used by the Cardiff City Council until the 1970s.*

three children and two lodgers. The mind boggles at the sleeping arrangements in such cramped quarters.

After the Public Health Report was accepted by the Cardiff Corporation, sweeping changes were made to improve the quality of life for the poorer citizens of the borough. However, such necessities as a proper water supply or decent sanitation were slow to arrive at Jones Court and places like it. The cottages were lit by candles and oil lamps and still lacked such a basic need as running water. Despite the primitive facilities, one resident remembered a neighbourly spirit: 'You never had to shut your front door, it was all so friendly'.

At that time, there were several pubs and a brewery in the vicinity of Jones Court. The Horse and Groom, the Model Inn and the City Arms survive today and are still busy pubs, especially when there is a big event at the Millennium Stadium. The Grand Theatre in Westgate Street provided entertainment in the form of melodrama. If the performance did not please the rowdy audience, the actors would be showered with a barrage of rotten fruit. A few yards away in Quay Street, Barton's mouth-watering faggots and peas were reputed to be 'the best ever made'.

In the late 19th century a massive house-building programme led to the construction of 20,000 houses in the new suburbs of Canton, Grangetown, Splott, Cathays and Roath. Gradually the courts of central Cardiff were demolished as families moved into better accommodation, but Jones Court was still occupied in 1892. At first it was used by the Cardiff Fire Brigade, but in 1896 the council

*Jones Court in 1977, when the houses were still more or less in their original form. At that time the cottages were being used by the refuse department as a dust-cart depot.*

purchased the site for £6,000. Throughout the next 70 years, the little court served as a workshop and store room for the lighting department before the cleansing department took over the premises as a storage depot for their dust carts.

The site remained a local curiosity, unknown to most people, even when it appeared on our television screens in the 1970s. When the BBC decided to film an

*Jones Court in 1990 following its restoration. It was the winner of the Prince of Wales award and is a fine example of conservation, but a complete contrast with the humble dwellings of nearly 200 years ago.*

adaptation of Jack Jones's famous novel *Off to Philadelphia in the Morning*, the producer used Jones Court to depict the humble background of young Joseph Parry, as nothing suitable could be found in his home town of Merthyr.

At that time, it occurred to the City Fathers that, despite its dilapidated appearance, Jones Court was a gem from Cardiff's past. There was talk of building

*The interior of one of the cottages at Jones Court in 1977. The hearth and chimney breast would have provided warmth but upstairs there was scarcely enough room to stand upright.*

an urban folk museum to complement that at St Fagans, while another proposal might have led to a Victorian restaurant and beer garden. A further possibility seemed to be an up-market shopping arcade. All these proposals had tourist potential but ultimately all came to naught. The corporation, pleading that it had no funds to do anything itself, gave its consent to the redevelopment of Jones Court. The work was carried out tastefully and won the Prince of Wales Award in 1982. The architects were the Cardiff-based firm of Lock-Necrews, Hill and Partners, while E. Turner and Sons were entrusted with the task of restoration. The company agreed to preserve the façade of the cottages while at the same time transforming them into offices.

Before work on the site began, a few people claim to have felt the presence of a ghost in the early hours of the morning. They spoke of an atmosphere of 'unbelievable cold' when entering one of the houses, while a door, which was barred and bolted, opened mysteriously when it was pushed.

It is an interesting thought that the houses of Jones Court, built for £1,000 in the 1830s, required more than £500,000 to complete the transformation into 15,000 square feet of offices. Three new blocks were added, one at each end of the court and another opposite the cottages. Inevitably they overshadow the 19th-century homes, but a genuine attempt was made to preserve their external appearance, using as much as possible of the existing materials. Even the lamp standards are original gas lamps belonging to the Cardiff Corporation and one even bears the city's coat of arms. Nevertheless, in looking at the splendid condition of these modern offices, it requires quite a feat of imagination to visualise the simple dwellings of those humble folk who lived in Jones Court little more than a hundred years ago.

## Chapter 6
# The Welsh Tsunami

Throughout the centuries the people of Cardiff were no strangers to flooding. In 1763, at the time of a spring tide, the moors of Canton were engulfed and hundreds of sheep were drowned. Another flood in 1791 caused such destruction south of the Town Quay that the west side of St Mary Street was virtually swept away. All traces of the old Town Wall and the houses along the river bank were obliterated. A year later severe flooding resulted in the partial collapse of Cardiff Bridge, causing great disruption to traffic.

*This scene of the Taff in flood was painted by Mrs Baden-Powell in 1840 and shows the river lapping the western side of St Mary Street. The bridge to the left of the picture preceded the present Cardiff Bridge.*

As late as 1806 the Taff was described as 'a rough and turbulent river' and coroners' inquests speak of numerous drownings in the river. Sometimes these were accidental, but often they were the result of incursions from the sea. In 1753 David John was riding home to Pendoylan. As he crossed the bridge at Cardiff over the Taff, 'the tide and flood being there, he was overpowered by the waters and carried down the said river to the Severn; and afterwards... was found drowned on the rocks in a certain place called Sully'.

*Many churches suffered severe damage in the Great Flood of 1607. Peterstone Wentloog, seen here in 1976, was one of them. The church is no longer used and is now a private residence.*

*On the wall of Peterstone Church, the date of the deluge is shown as 20 January 1606. This is not an error, as in those days the ecclesiastical and legal year began on 25 March.*

Bad as these incidents were, they seem almost insignificant compared with the Great Flood of 1607, the worst natural disaster ever to strike Britain, much more devastating than the east-coast floods of 1953. A few miles to the east of Cardiff, there are stark reminders of this tragedy, such as the memorial stone on the east wall of the former church at Peterstone Wentloog. Not far away, in the porch of St Brides Church, a tablet simply reads 'The great flud, 20 Ianuarie, in the morning, 1606'. A couple of miles further along the coast at Goldcliff, a brass plate reveals that 22 parishioners died as a result of the disaster.

There are a number of contemporary accounts of this catastrophe, which affected the entire coastline of the Bristol Channel but particularly the counties of Somerset, Glamorgan and Monmouthshire. Throughout the region 200 square miles of land were permanently swallowed up by the sea and hundreds of houses were destroyed. Both the English and the Welsh coastlines of the Bristol Channel were submerged and so deep was the flood in places that the steeples of churches were almost hidden from view.

On the Welsh side of the channel, an area 24 miles long and four miles wide was covered by a surging torrent in less than five hours. A description of the carnage in South Wales is written by an unknown chronicler who recorded the 'Strange and Wonderful Overflowing of Waters' in a pamphlet entitled *Wofull Newes*

from Wales. The coastal plain that lay to the east of Cardiff was the most gravely affected region. Among the 26 parishes of Monmouthshire, 'spoiled by the grievous and lamentable fury of the waters', were St Mellons, St Brides, Peterstone, Rumney and Marshfield.

*St Bride's Church was another to face the full fury of the deluge. The memorial in the porch has not been kindly treated by the passage of time but is just about readable.*

There was no sign of what was to come in the early morning of Tuesday 20 January 1607. The day began brightly enough, but soon after nine o'clock, without any warning, a wall of water swept up the Severn 'with a swiftness so incredible that no greyhound could have escaped by running before it'. In another broadsheet, entitled *God's Warning to His People of England,* the chronicler graphically wrote 'huge and mighty hills of water were tumbling one over another in such sort as if the greatest mountains in the world had overwhelmed the low villages or marshy grounds'. Smoke appeared to be billowing from these mountains as though they were on fire. The writer goes on to say: 'To the view of some it seemed as if millions of thousands of arrows had been shot all at one time', ricocheting like sparks off the waves.

For the poor people affected by this mighty force of nature there was no warning. The eventual death toll was more than 2,000. The speed of the disaster gave people no time to take evasive action and those who survived the initial shock stood little chance of living more than a few minutes if they were flung into the freezing January waters. Neither tall trees nor high ground provided a guarantee of safety. Those who thought they were safe were sadly mistaken. Mistress Van, 'a gentlewoman of good sort', lived four miles from the sea. She saw the waves advancing towards her but, before she could reach the safety of her upper rooms, she was drowned.

In the midst of all this chaos, there were tales of miraculous escapes. A man and woman who had climbed a tree saw the deluge about to engulf them, when a large tub floated towards them and gently nestled against the tree. Hastily they took advantage of this gift, which now became their lifeboat. A mother, unable to save herself, placed her naked four-year-old daughter on a beam in the roof and, as the water rushed in, a chicken flew up to join her and so, 'by the heat thereof… preserved the childe's life in the middest of so colde a tempest'. Another child was found in a cradle with only a cat to keep him company. When the cradle was floating to the shore, the cat could be seen leaping from side to side as if it had been 'appointed steersman to preserve the small barque from the waves' fury'.

Tens of thousands of cattle and sheep lay dead in the waters. On the higher

# WOFULL NEWES FROM WALES.

### OR

*The lamentable* losse *of divers* Villages *and* Parishes (*by a* strange *and* wonderfull Floud) *within the Countye of* Monmouth *in* Wales; *Which hapned in* January last past 1607. *whereby a great number of his* Ma^ties *Subjects, Inhabiting in those partes, are* utterlye *undone.*

THE holye Scriptures teacheth us, that when as God had framed the Heavens, Earth, Sea, Aire and all that in them is, hee then created Mankinde the last of all : even as it were a little briefe or concise Mappe, a summe or an abridge- f whole weldes perfections to the intent, that beholding so soone as h

ground at Llandaff, some miles from the sea, Mistress Matthews lost 400 ewes. Wild animals who had survived the onslaught were so frightened they made no attempt to prey on one another. One observer spoke of terrified rabbits desperately clinging to the backs of sheep in an attempt to escape.

Ten days passed before the flood began to recede and, even after the waters had

subsided, it was many years before some of the fields and meadows ruined by the salt could once again be cultivated. In Monmouthshire alone, the value of the ruined land was put at £40,000 and the total cost of the carnage amounted to £100,000, a huge sum in those days. Many of those who survived the mountainous wall of water were homeless and perished in its aftermath, either from the winter weather or for want of food. Others, who might have been considered prosperous when they woke that morning, found themselves reduced to poverty. Inevitably there were rogues who sought to profit from the tragedy. If they had boats, they took the opportunity to steal livestock drifting in the water.

Other people responded with compassion. Local landowners and gentry, among them Lord Herbert of Cardiff Castle and Sir Walter Montague, brother to the Recorder of London, tried to relieve the distress caused by the flood. They dispatched boats to rescue people and distributed food and clothing to the survivors where it was possible to reach them.

Few records have survived to indicate the impact of the flood on the town of Cardiff, but most of the borough would certainly have been under water. We know that St Mary's Church was hastened to its doom by the fury of the storm. Poorly sited on low-lying land at the south end of St Mary Street, it had suffered from earlier floods, but in 1607 the writer of *God's Warning* claims that 'a great part of the church… was beaten down with the water'. John Speed's plan of Cardiff in 1610 shows that a corner of the churchyard had disappeared, and he observed that the Taff was 'a foe of St Mary's Church… undermining her foundations and threatening her fall'. Services were to continue at the church for a few more years, but it is true to say that St Mary's never recovered from the disaster and was abandoned before the end of the century.

Like many others, the chronicler of *Wofull Newes from Wales* was under no illusions that the flood was a warning from God. It was a reminder 'that the Lord useth from time to time, to reveal his wrath from heaven', as the writer compared this catastrophe with the story of Noah's Ark. The tragedy has become part of local folklore as anecdotes were passed down from one generation to another. One of the more macabre tales recalls that 200 bodies, half buried in the silt as the waters subsided, were found about half a mile from Marshfield.

For a long time a freak wave was thought to be the most likely explanation for this catastrophe. The tide that morning was one of the most massive on record and it was accompanied by a violent wind from the south-west that whipped up the waves. More recently geologists have detected fault lines below the Atlantic Ocean off the west coast of Ireland. These appear to suggest that what happened in 1607 was a tsunami, not unlike that which occurred in the Indian Ocean in 2004.

*A horseman and a milk cart plough through the water near Mardy Road in Rumney after heavy rain caused flooding in 1931. This was part of the region that suffered a far worse fate 300 years earlier.*

Sand and shells alien to South Wales have been deposited against the cliffs along the Bristol Channel, while at Dunraven huge boulders, seven tons or more in weight, appear to have been hurled on to the shore as though they were pebbles. It is quite possible that these happenings were caused by a volcanic upheaval in the Atlantic, which lifted the ocean floor and produced a mountainous wave travelling at 100mph. Whatever was the cause of this disaster, it certainly had the same impact as a tsunami.

Cardiff continued to have its problems as the Taff burst its banks from time to time. Matters improved in 1849 when Isambard Kingdom Brunel was planning the route of the South Wales Railway through Cardiff and the Town Council persuaded him to divert the course of the river 200 metres to the west.

Yet, even in the 20th century, there were a number of floods which caused a great deal of damage in Cardiff. Canton, Riverside and Grangetown were some of the districts of the city that often lay under water when the level of the Taff rose after heavy rain. One of the worst floods occurred in November 1927, when the River Ely burst its banks and the much loved Billy the Seal departed from his pool in Victoria Park. The story of his travels has passed into folklore, immortalised and embellished by Frank Hennessy in song. It relates how Billy swam down Cowbridge Road, stopping along the way for fish and chips and a pint of 'Brains' Dark' before returning home.

*Serious flooding continued to be a problem in Cardiff during the 20th century. After heavy rain in December 1960, Cowbridge Road resembled a tributary of the Taff rather than the main thoroughfare through Canton.*

As you look out to sea from the shore near Peterstone Church today, it is usually a tranquil scene far removed from the terror of that awful January morning in 1607. Recently I visited the area after heavy rain. The day was dull and wet and the sea was sullen and grey, but the stout sea wall, at least 10 feet high and equally wide, had held firm.

The last time there was serious flooding in Cardiff was in 1979, and 15 years later the Welsh Office announced spending plans of £4 million to strengthen the sea defences of South Wales. The defences would be strong enough, it was said, to withstand the worst possible disaster, the kind that occurs once in a thousand years. Hopefully the experts are right and the horrors of the Welsh Tsunami will remain a unique page in our history.

**Further reading:**
**Anon** *Wofull Newes From Wales*, London, 1891.
**Waters, B.** *The Bristol Channel* pp18–20, J.M. Dent & Sons, 1955.

*The flat landscape of St Mellons has changed little since the district was inundated in the flood of 1607. Could the much improved sea defences of today withstand a similar disaster?*

## Chapter 7
# The West Gate

The West Gate, near the Clock Tower of Cardiff Castle, was restored by the fourth Marquess of Bute in 1921. On it is a blue plaque, which reminds us that this was once the site of the western entrance into Cardiff. Local records first mention the West Gate in 1184 when the Town Walls were no more than a wooden palisade, built by Robert, Earl of Gloucester, in 1111. The gate was integrated into the defences of the town and was one of the five entrances within the mediaeval wall surrounding the town. In the 13th century Gilbert de Clare rebuilt walls and gates of the town in stone as a precautionary measure. At the time Llywelyn ap Gruffydd, the Prince of Gwynedd, who nursed ambitions to be master of the whole of Wales, was advancing into Glamorgan.

*The blue plaque on the West Gate was donated by the* South Wales Echo *in 1975. Unfortunately it was damaged during recent work at the castle but, despite its present condition, it gives an outline of the part it has played in the history of Cardiff.*

Originally there were no domestic buildings to the west of the castle and the Lords of Glamorgan and their retainers lived in the strongly reinforced keep. When visitors entered the town through the West Gate, the castle walls lay about 50 yards ahead. Enemy forces, even if they could fight their way through the gate, would still find themselves con-fronting a wall, lined with defenders capable of hurling arrows and other missiles at them.

The West Gate was sometimes referred to as 'Sentry House', but it was more commonly known as the 'Mill Gate'. There were two mills just outside the entrance where, after paying a toll to the Lord of Glamorgan, the townspeople were able to grind their corn into flour. Two gatekeepers, one of whom lived above the West Gate, were responsible for closing the gates at curfew in the evening and re-opening them in the morning. The payment for this task was 2d a day and a

*By the 18th century the West Gate had ceased to be an integral part of the castle's defences. This peaceful scene reflects that tranquillity as a horseman rides through the gate and bystanders exchange pleasantries.*

peal of bells from St John's Church informed the people of Cardiff when these duties were being carried out.

Mediaeval travellers approached the West Gate from the ancient Roman road through Ely and Canton. They caught their first glimpse of the gate and the castle when they arrived at Cardiff Bridge, which was about 80 yards further upstream than it is today. It was no more than a flimsy timber structure, which was occasionally swept away by flood. Whenever this happened, travellers were forced to make a lengthy detour around Llandaff. In 1580 the bridge was rebuilt in stone for the first time and was used for over 200 years. It survived some damage during the Civil War but serious flooding in 1792 led to its partial collapse. Four years later a new bridge was constructed near the site of the present Cardiff Bridge, which was built in 1859.

Over the years, armies have marched out of the West Gate into battle and adversaries have attacked it in an attempt to force their way into the town. No assault upon Cardiff was more serious than that of 1404 when Owain Glyndwr was rampaging through Wales. The Glyndwr Revolt began in 1400 as a boundary dispute in Denbighshire between Owain and his neighbour, Reginald de Grey. King Henry IV lent his support to Grey, and the dispute soon erupted into a major rebellion that engulfed the whole of the Principality. Every resentment the Welsh

had been nursing for years against their English conquerors now expressed itself under the charismatic leadership of this man who claimed the title, 'Prince of Wales'. Welshmen flocked to serve under him, and at one stage he ruled virtually all of Wales apart from Pembroke Castle and the great Edwardian castles of Gwynedd. In 1403 Owain advanced into Glamorgan, where Anglo-Norman influence was particularly strong, and the following year he fell upon Llandaff 'like a second Assyrian, the rod of God's anger'. While Llandaff Cathedral was spared, the Bishop's Castle and the Bell Tower were reduced to a shell.

Next it was the turn of Cardiff, the stronghold of the Lord of Glamorgan, to feel Owain's wrath. The plaque on the West Gate recalls how he stormed into the town and proceeded to systematically plunder the borough. Houses and shops, whether they were made of wood or stone, were gutted in an orgy of destruction. Nor were the churches and friaries spared, and the priory of St Mary's Church was completely wrecked. Excavations at the Blackfriars' site near the West Gate indicate that some of the tiles had been blackened by fire during the Glyndwr Revolt. Presumably Owain believed the Dominican friars were unsympathetic to his cause.

Only the convent of the Greyfriars was left intact, as they had been among Owain's most loyal supporters elsewhere in Wales. He left their friary unharmed 'out of the love he bore them', but rather foolishly they had placed their treasures in the security of Cardiff Castle. Owain, now master of the castle, chided them: 'wherefore did you place your goods in the castle? If you had kept them in your convent they would have been safe'. It is not clear whether he returned their valuables or not. Owain's success was not destined to last and, as the tide of battle turned against him, he disappeared and his memory faded into the mists of legend. Now that Cardiff is the capital of Wales, Owain has been forgiven for the havoc he wreaked in the town. His statue at the City Hall shows him in defiant pose among the great figures of Welsh history.

However, the walls of Cardiff were so severely damaged that 100 years later a

*This fine view of Cardiff from the north-west in 1748 was the work of Samuel and Nathaniel Buck. The engraving shows the road across the bridge of the Taff, leading towards the town.*

*Alfred Turner designed this statue of Owain Glyndwr which stands in the City Hall. It is a fitting tribute to a great Welsh hero, but signs of the devastation he caused in Cardiff in 1404 were still visible a century later.*

*Even in the 21st century the machicolation of the Beauchamp Tower presents a sinister appearance. These holes could be used to pour hot sand or boiling water on an enemy attacking the walls below.*

levy was still being imposed on traders to pay for their repair. Contemporary accounts describe buildings in Cardiff as valueless after being 'burnt by the rebel Welsh'. All the gates were wrecked in the onslaught, and the Lord of Glamorgan decided that not only the West Gate needed rebuilding but also the western defences of the castle. Rather belatedly Richard Neville, the Earl of Warwick, built the massive Octagonal Tower, using every defensive ploy known at that time, including machicolation or 'murder holes'. At the same time a range of domestic quarters, including the Great Hall, was built along the West Wall.

The new tower was not required to repel any further attacks from the Welsh, but the West Gate was to bear witness to another conflict in the 17th century. Cardiff Castle saw little fighting in the Civil War, though it was of strategic importance to both sides. In the opening stages of the war, the Royalists were able to capture the stronghold in a bloodless coup and for three years the castle remained a royal garrison. By 1646 the fortunes of war had swung in favour of Parliament and some of the local gentry decided it was prudent to change sides. Soon afterwards, Charles I was taken prisoner, and it seemed that the Civil War was over, though a garrison of Cromwell's army remained at the castle.

In 1648 a new threat emerged as a Royalist army marched upon Cardiff from the west with the intention of seizing the castle before joining other Royalist

*In 1648 Cromwell's Model Army set forth from the West Gate to fight the Battle of St Fagans. The event was commemorated 350 years later at the Museum of Welsh Life when the Sealed Knot Society re-enacted the battle.*

sympathisers in England. As the plaque informs us, Parliament forces marched out of the West Gate to link up with another detachment moving south from the Rhondda. When the crucial Battle of St Fagans was fought near Peterston on the cold, wet morning of 8 May 1648, the Royalists were no match for the well-disciplined troops of Cromwell's New Model Army and were routed in just two hours. The battle was the most important to be fought in Wales during the Civil War and signalled the end of the King's attempt to regain his throne.

*Paul Sandby published this print in 1777, shortly before the West Gate was demolished. There is a homely domestic touch as one woman washes her clothes in the moat while another hangs her washing on the line.*

*The West Gate of today is less than a century old but it acts as a reminder of the days when its predecessor was of vital importance to the borough's commerce and defence.*

The Civil War was the last time the West Gate played a part in the defence of Cardiff. A print of the castle and West Gate in the 18th century shows a peaceful scene as a horseman approaches the moat. The mighty Octagonal Tower is the dominant feature in the picture and the Town Mills are still standing near the gate. In 1781 the council decided that the gate was obstructing traffic into the town and ordered its demolition. During the next 20 years, all the mediaeval gates of Cardiff were removed.

What was once a bustling hive of activity around the West Gate became peaceful parkland in the 19th century. About the same time, William Burges transformed the western skyline of the castle as he created his Victorian masterpiece. Three new towers were built, but the Beauchamp Tower is still easily identified, despite Burges's decision to enhance it with a lead spire. The present West Gate is mostly a modern reproduction, though part of the original remains. The cobbled road leading to it over the bridge creates a nostalgic atmosphere from the past, when the rumbling of carts, the neighing of horses and the cries of street vendors were everyday sounds as the traffic flowed into mediaeval Cardiff.

**Further reading:**

**Rees, W.** *Cardiff, A History of the City*, Cardiff Corporation, 1969.
**Grant, J.P.** *Cardiff Castle – Its History and Architecture*, Cardiff, 1923.

*Chapter 8*
# The Fate of the Greyfriars
# and the Blackfriars

There are few traces of the two friaries which once played a prominent part in the religious life of Cardiff. In Bute Park, not far from the river, lie the scanty remains of the Blackfriars' Convent. Where the Greyfriars once worshipped, all archaeological evidence has vanished. They are remembered only by two plaques, one of which has disappeared, and two street names: 'The Friary' and 'Greyfriars Road'.

The Blackfriars, so called because of the black cloaks they wore over their white, woollen robes, were founded by St Dominic, an imperious Spaniard who dedicated his life to stamping out heresy. In accordance with these aims, the Dominicans placed great emphasis on prayer, study and discipline. They were worthy, pious men, contributing a great deal to the intellectual life of the times and upholding the dignity of the Church. However, with their aloof, aristocratic manner, they did not find it easy to capture the hearts of the common folk who held them in some awe. The ritual of their daily life began at 2am when the first of seven services during the day was held. The sick rose from their beds to join in the devotions, though if they had an infectious disease they sat

*This plaque, which relates the story of the Greyfriars, was originally presented by Helical Bar in June 1997. The firm no longer occupies the premises and unfortunately this record of the site has been lost. Attempts are being made to replace it.*

apart from the rest of the congregation. The Dominicans were welcomed to Cardiff in 1242 by Richard de Clare, the Lord of Glamorgan. He granted them a site, between the West Gate and the river, to build their convent.

The Franciscans, or Greyfriars, arrived in Cardiff about 40 years later. They were much more popular than the austere Dominicans, especially among the poor. Their founder was St Francis of Assisi, one of the most gentle, saintly and loveable men who ever walked the earth. Wearing their rough, coarse tunics of brownish-grey cloth, the Franciscans renounced worldly wealth and believed that a life of poverty would bring them closer to God. It was Richard's son, Gilbert de Clare, who provided them with land outside the Town Walls, near the North and East Gates, from which they could carry out their work.

The earliest friaries would have been simple structures of wood, wattle and clay. In time something more durable was erected and both the convents in Cardiff appear to have been rebuilt in stone by the early 14th century. The Clares were noted for their generosity to the friars and provided the building materials, while the townspeople were willing assistants in the task of construction. At both friaries there were cloisters where the brethren could walk and meditate in silence. Each establishment had its own chapter house where the friars met to discuss the duties and administration of their orders. The infirmary was another essential building in an age when disease and plague were everyday perils in the community.

*Spring flowers bloom in Bute Park, where once there was a thriving community. These footments are now all that remain of the buildings that were a part of the Blackfriars' Convent.*

Both friaries were excavated by the Marquess of Bute in 1887, and the results of his investigations at the Blackfriars site can still be seen in Bute Park. Only fragments remain from most of the buildings, but the foundations of a large church are clearly defined. Some of its floor tiles were decorated with pictures of birds and horsemen. Stained glass from the 14th century, multi-coloured with illustrations of animals, birds and flowers, was also found. While excavations were taking place, the tomb of John Ecclescliffe, who was bishop of Llandaff from 1323 until 1346, was discovered. An examination of his grave revealed a well-preserved skeleton in a lead coffin, but at some point it had been pillaged by grave robbers, no doubt searching for his ring and chalice, both of which would have been buried with him.

A plan prior to the construction of Greyfriars Road shows the layout of the Franciscan Convent. The burial ground lay to the south of the church and domestic buildings were arranged around a cloister to the north. Any traces of these buildings would have been extinguished when Greyfriars Road was opened in 1928, but they would have included the refectory and kitchen, a guest room, the friars' dormitory and their chapter house. The main entrance to the convent was through a stone archway in Crockerton Street, or Queen Street as it later became. The gate was demolished when St John's National School was built in 1819.

*The grave of John Ecclescliffe, who died in 1347, lay in the choir of the Blackfriars' Church. Formerly the Bishop of Connor in Ireland, the Pope appointed Ecclescliffe as Bishop of Llandaff in 1323.*

A path across the graveyard led to the 14th-century church of St Francis, the main door of which faced the town. The church was a large building of five or six bays with a steeple at its east end. This housed a single bell to call the friars to their devotions. When the site was excavated, the columns of the church were marked with brick emplacements, and it was seen that the choir was at a slightly higher level than the nave. It was thought possible that stained glass might have been used to decorate the windows of the church.

About 30 skeletons were discovered while archaeological work was proceeding. One of them was that of Llywelyn Bren, a famous Welsh folk hero of the early 14th century, who led a rebellion against cruel oppression by the Lord of Glamorgan. For two years the villages and hamlets around Cardiff were aflame with battle. Even mighty Caerphilly Castle was besieged, but eventually Llywelyn succumbed to superior forces and surrendered to the King. He was hung, drawn and quartered outside the Black Tower of Cardiff Castle. Afterwards the Greyfriars gathered up what was left of his body and laid it in a wooden tomb inside their church. To the local people, Llywelyn was a martyr and the readiness of the Franciscans to grant him a Christian burial did much to endear them to the Welsh people. Ironically, Sir William Fleming, the sheriff who had supervised the execution, later suffered the same fate as Llywelyn, and he too was buried at the Greyfriars' Church.

Neither of the Cardiff friaries was ever rich, but they were both self-sufficient and each of them tilled a few acres of land. The Greyfriars cultivated fields and gardens to the north of the friary where the civic centre now stands. Two of these meadows, containing a stable and a barn, were known as Cow Close and Friars' Close.

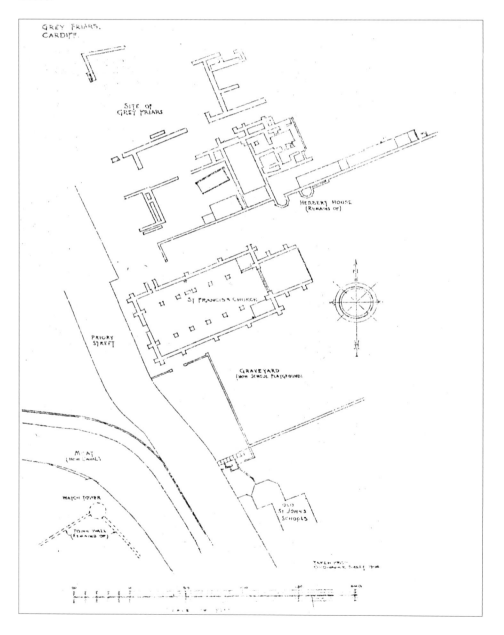

*Revd J.M. Cronin's plan of the Greyfriars site and Herbert House in the 1920s. At that time St John's National School was still open and its playground backed on to the former graveyard of the friary.*

The friars were respected by local clergy and were often invited to preach at the Churches of St Mary's or St John's. Their convents were no more than a lodging from which they could venture forth and reach out to the people. This was particularly true of the Greyfriars, who were prepared to preach wherever a congregation could be found. It

The architect, George Robinson, drew this sketch of the entrance to the Greyfriars. A note on the sketch states: 'This gateway was pulled down when St John's schools were erected; it was then used as a wheelwright's shop and smithy'.

might be in the villages near Cardiff, at the Town Cross in High Street on Market Day or at the annual fairs in June and September. Their services were happy affairs and the call to repent was always accompanied by singing and music.

Four of the Franciscans became Bishops of Llandaff and one of them, John Zouche, was buried in the Greyfriars' Church. It was concern for the outcasts of society that endeared the Greyfriars to the common people. They brought help and comfort to those in need and, in many respects, their work resembled that of the modern Salvation Army. Near their convent was the Spital, the former leper hospital in Crockerton and, in an age of dreadful diseases, they toiled among the sick. During the Black Death of 1348–49, in which nearly half the population of the country perished, the Greyfriars suffered considerably. As poor wretches lay dying in the streets, priests and doctors were afraid to approach them in case they caught the disease. In Cardiff, as elsewhere, the Franciscans stayed with the afflicted and, in doing so, they often sacrificed their lives.

Herbert House and the Greyfriars' Church in the late 19th century after the site had been excavated. The tiles were not part of the original floor but were placed there during the excavation.

89

*The foundations of the Franciscan Church and the remains of the friary in 1928, the year Greyfriars Road was opened. St John's School lies to the right of the photograph.*

For 300 years the brothers were a familiar sight in Cardiff and the surrounding countryside. Their numbers reached a peak in about 1300 when there were 18 Franciscan and 30 Dominican friars in the town. Thereafter, following the Black Death, their numbers began to decline and, after the Glyndwr Revolt, neither of the Cardiff friaries prospered again. In other parts of the country, the friars accumulated great wealth, and their corruption and greed became so notorious that it was said a traveller feared to meet a friar as much as a robber. The collection of alms was almost turned into a business and tales were told of friars who preyed on the dying in their search for money. Even the Franciscans were no longer true to the high ideals of their founder and, when Henry VIII decided to seize the wealth of the monasteries and friaries, he met with little resistance.

Accusations of greed and materialism could certainly not be levelled against either the Dominicans or the Franciscans in Cardiff. Few endowments were given to them and they held little property in the town apart from their convents. Small bequests, such as the £6 left in her will by Elizabeth de Clare in 1360, were infrequent. Sometimes cattle and sheep were given as gifts in kind, and the Greyfriars drew a small rent from land they possessed on the marshy moors near the sea. In 1487, in a petition to the Pope, the Franciscans claimed their house was in a ruinous state of repair and their poverty was forcing them to travel ever more widely in their search for alms and food. Inevitably, the influence of the Cardiff friaries on society was reduced, and they shared the fate of friars and monks elsewhere.

In 1538 the King's visitor, Richard Ingworth, who was himself an ex-Dominican priest, was given the authority 'to visit and vex the friaries of Wales'.

In theory, this meant that his task was to seize their chattels and depose any friar who did not accept the new decrees which Henry had imposed as Head of the Church. In reality, such conditions left the brothers with no alternative but to yield everything to the Crown.

On 6 September Ingworth arrived in Cardiff and the Blackfriars were the first to receive the royal visitor. The setting could hardly have been more dismal. Only seven of the brethren remained to witness this final chapter in their history and, as the bell summoned them to the chapter house, they were all in mourning. Three of their companions, including their prior, had passed away 10 days earlier. Ingworth had little difficulty in extracting surrender from this shattered community and, 'without any manner of coercion or counsel', the friars signed the deed disposing of their property. They possessed very little of value and even owed a local victualler for the food they had recently purchased. A few items were sold to pay their debts and Ingworth felt justified in retaining the one item of real value, a silver chalice, to pay for his personal expenses.

A few hours later the bell tolled at the Franciscan Church as Ingworth presented his demands to the nine remaining friars. After listening to his ultimatum, they obediently surrendered their convent to the King, while 'desiring his grace to be good and gracious to us'. They had a few silver ornaments, which were weighed and despatched to London to be sold on behalf of the Crown.

There was nothing gracious about the way in which the friars were subsequently treated. Unlike monks, who were sometimes given a pension when they were expelled from their monasteries, the friars were turned penniless into the world. Men who had known nothing but the life of a religious community did not find it easy to find alternative work at a time of high unemployment. The more elderly brethren probably had to beg for the rest of their lives.

The furnishings and valuables from the friaries, meagre as they were, had already disappeared to swell the royal coffers. The King's Commissioners ordered a local administrator, Lewis Bleddyn, to sell the stone, glass, timber and tiles from the two buildings. Some of the stone was used to repair the castle walls in 1589 but inevitably local people looted the deserted buildings at night, and many a home or business in Cardiff was renovated with materials from the two sites. In 1655 William Jones was accused of removing 40 wagon loads of stone, thatch and timber from the convent of the Blackfriars, as well as numerous tiles, beams and rafters. This particular act of plunder was investigated by the Sheriff, but there is no record of any action being taken against the culprit.

Within a few years both convents had lapsed into a state of ruin. Speed's map of Cardiff in 1610 shows the shell of two buildings, one without a roof, where the Dominican Friary had stood. Before the industrial pollution of the 19th century, the Taff was still a river teeming with fish and what remained of the friary was

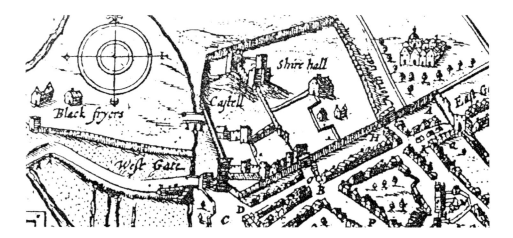

rented as cottages to fishermen. Their coracles, fishing for salmon and trout, were a familiar sight on the river as late as 1840 before these buildings were finally demolished.

Both friaries were put up for sale and were purchased in 1546 by George Herbert of Swansea. The Franciscans' Convent was destroyed before the end of the century, and in 1578 Rhys Merrick, a local historian from Cottrell near St Nicholas, referred to, 'the Gray ffriars, wherein Sir William Herbert, Knight, hath builded a house of late'. Sir William, the grandson of George Herbert, had used the materials from the friary to build a fine mansion with four high gables, high pitched roofs and Tudor bay windows. It was known locally as 'The Friars' and only the castle was a larger building in Cardiff. The Friars remained the town house of the Herbert family until the 18th century, but, after the death of an infant heir, a dispute between two female heiresses led to bitter legal arguments. By 1746

*Fishing on the Taff in the 18th century. The cottages on the left were either the last buildings to survive from the Blackfriars' Convent or were built with stone taken from it.*

*The Herbert family lived at 'The Friars' until about 1735 but, as the house became the subject of a lawsuit, it was abandoned soon afterwards. By 1805 'The Friars' was lapsing into a crumbling ruin.*

*The proposal to build a Roman Catholic cathedral on the Greyfriars site was abandoned by the fourth Marquess because of its cost. This design by the architects, Kempson and Fowler, indicates how the church might have appeared if the plan had reached fruition.*

the Herberts had departed from Cardiff and the house, no longer occupied, fell into ruin and decay.

It presented a rather sinister presence at night and, according to a local legend, the precincts were haunted by spirits. Perhaps they were the ghosts of the friars, but one spectre, known as 'Bully Dean', was particularly frightening. In 1737 the magistrates heard how John Price of Cardiff had assaulted a girl. While having his wicked way he warned her that if she cried out Bully Dean and the other spirits would appear from the friary and carry her off.

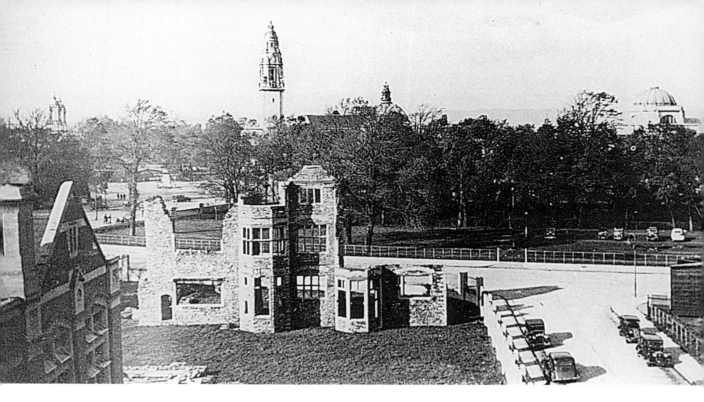

*Herbert House and Greyfriars Road in 1935. The civic centre is much quieter than it is today with just a few cars parked in The Friary and across the road. The building to the right is Blogg's School of Commerce.*

*Capital Towers in Cathays Park. The skyscraper was originally built by John Morgan for the Pearl Assurance Company in the 1960s. Its construction resulted in the demise of one of Cardiff's most notable historical sites.*

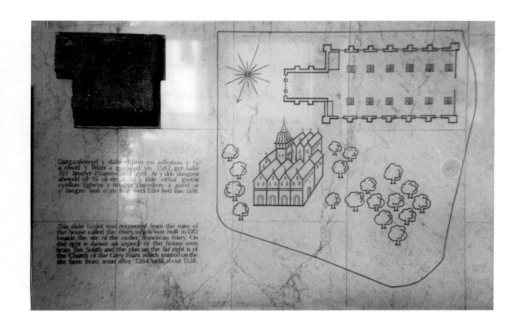

*Inside Capital Towers is a memorial tablet, giving a brief history of the friary and Herbert House. At present the name 'Greyfriars Road' is the only other reminder of the Franciscan brothers who once worshipped there.*

In the 18th century ownership of the site passed to the Bute family. In 1897 the third Marquess contemplated building a Roman Catholic cathedral on the site, an idea that would certainly have been preferable to its ultimate fate. As late as the 1960s, Herbert House and the remains of the friary were one of the few ancient monuments still remaining in Cardiff. Unfortunately, the land was considered much too valuable to be left in its existing state and the site was sold to the Pearl Assurance Company. The bulldozers moved in to obliterate the ancient ruins and a 25-storey tower block of glass, concrete and steel took its place. As it rose above the castle and the civic centre, the managing director of the building firm commented: 'There were fears that it might spoil the general appearance of the area, but we are convinced it will add to, rather than detract from, the appearance of the district'. To this day, few people in Cardiff agree, although, just inside Capital Towers, as the building is now known, an attractive memorial reminds us of the gentle Franciscans who once worshipped here.

**Further reading:**
**Morgan, D.** *The Cardiff Story*, Dennis Morgan, 1991.
**Cronin, J.M.** *The Cardiff Greyfriars*, Priory Press, 1924.
**Chappell, E.L.** *Cardiff's Civic Centre*, Priory Press 1946.

# Chapter 9
# The Town Halls of Cardiff

A plaque on the wall of Zizzi's restaurant in High Street marks the site of the first two town halls in Cardiff, both of which were erected in the middle of High Street facing towards the castle. The plot of land on which they were built was granted to the burgesses of the town by William Zouche, the Lord of Glamorgan, in 1331.

There is no pictorial record of the first Town Hall apart from a rather vague illustration on John Speed's map of 1610. However, we do have a description of it in 1578 from Rice Merrick, who wrote that in High Street 'standeth a faire Towne Hall, wherein is holden the Town Court, every ffortnight'. From Merrick's account, it seems likely that the building was similar to one that still stands in Llantwit Major, another town which was under the governance of the Lord of Glamorgan.

In 1338 the Cardiff Corporation met for the first time at its new Town Hall in the 'great chamber on the upper storey'. This acted both as a courtroom and a meeting place where the Council could conduct its business. The charter, which Hugh Despenser granted to Cardiff in 1340, allowed the burgesses to elect their representatives to the Council, but later charters, including those bestowed by the Crown, took away this privilege. Instead councillors were chosen from a select group of 12 aldermen, and for centuries Cardiff's local government was in the hands of a small clique with the power to appoint its own nominees. It was not until 1835 that the Municipal Corporations Act prescribed elections every three years in which ratepayers, whose annual rent exceeded £10, had the right to vote.

The Town Hall was a focal point for commercial activity, and on market days the surrounding area became a beehive of activity.

MEDIAEVAL & GEORGIAN TOWN HALLS

THE FIRST TOWN HALL, KNOWN ALSO AS BOTHALL, GUILDHALL OR TOWN HOUSE, WAS BUILT c.1338 FACING THE CASTLE ON A SITE IN THE CENTRE OF HIGH STREET GRANTED BY THE LORD, WILLIAM LA ZOUCHE. IN 1578 IT WAS DESCRIBED BY RHYS MERRICK (RHYS MEURIG) AS COMPRISING A GREAT CHAMBER ABOVE FOR COURT AND MUNICIPAL BUSINESS AND A SHAMBLES (MEAT-MARKET) AND CWCHMOEL (PRISON) BELOW. TO THE REAR WERE THE TOWN CROSS AND STOCKS. A TURRET, TOWN BELL AND CLOCK (PRESERVED) WERE ADDED LATER. REBUILT IN 1742-7 IN GEORGIAN STYLE BUT MAJOR REPAIRS REQUIRED BY 1774. REPLACED BY ST MARY STREET TOWN HALL IN 1854. USED FOR OTHER MUNICIPAL PURPOSES UNTIL DEMOLITION IN 1861. STATUE OF SECOND MARQUESS OF BUTE ERECTED IN FRONT IN 1853; MOVED TO THE MONUMENT SITE AT THE SOUTH END OF ST MARY STREET IN 1879.

DONATED BY LLOYDS BANK PLC, NOVEMBER 1993

The building was also a meeting place for the guilds and was often known as the Booth Hall or the Guild Hall. All the different craftsmen and traders had their own organisation to control the commercial life of the town. The power of the guilds was enormous. They eliminated competition by fixing the prices of their goods, decided the conditions of apprenticeship and ensured that no newcomer to the town could practise his craft until he was accepted into the guild. Heavy fines were imposed on anyone who dared to break the rules. Not until the late 18th century, when public opinion at last refused to accept such restraints on trade, did the guilds finally lose their privileges.

The Town Cross stood at the crossroads to the south of the Town Hall, where Quay Street and Church Street join High Street. Merrick describes it as, 'a faire Crosse… covered with lead'. The cross was a reminder that God was watching while burgesses repaid their debts and merchants exchanged contracts or haggled over business transactions.

In those days, when news was slow to travel, the Town Crier would take up his position outside the Town Hall on market days. Amid the babble around him, he

*The mediaeval town hall at Llantwit Major was built in the 15th century, somewhat later than Cardiff's first Town Hall. However, it is likely that the buildings are of similar design.*

needed a stentorian voice to communicate news of national and local events. He would also issue decrees of the Council such as the need to control animals in the streets or the necessity for greater cleanliness in the town. Whether such edicts were heeded was another matter. The Town Crier remained an important figure in everyday life until the early 19th century. In October 1788 council records show a payment of 6d to Christopher Phillips, a man with a voice so powerful that he was known as 'the best ever among Cardiff's criers'.

*Cardiff's second Town Hall has been illustrated by several artists. This is an imaginative portrayal which can be seen in the St David's Shopping Centre at the entrance to Marks & Spencer.*

1750 CARDIFF TOWN HALL WITH DOCKS BEYOND

Market Day on 30 March 1555 would have been a more restrained affair than usual. On that day the Protestant martyr Rawlins White was burnt at the stake near the Town Hall. Prior to his execution, he had been held in the 'very dark, loathsome and most vile prison', known as the Cwchmoel. This Welsh expression was another term for the tiny, poky cell on the ground floor of the Town Hall. Its normal use was to detain those who owed debts or were guilty of public order offences.

Outside the Town Hall were the stocks and the pillory. These were the deterrents for petty criminals. A few hours in the stocks on Market Day was the punishment meted out to such rogues as the brewer who sold sour beer or the baker who put sawdust in his bread. The stocks were used as a form of punishment well into the 19th century and were not finally removed until the second Town Hall was pulled down in 1861.

Cardiff's first Town Hall stood in High Street for over 400 years. By 1741 councillors concluded that repairing the dilapidated state of the building would be so costly that the only solution was to replace it. The decision to build a new Town Hall in the same place is surprising in view of many complaints about the obstruction to traffic. Somewhat optimistically, the council asked the more

*The Golden Cross Hotel has some interesting murals of important buildings relating to Cardiff's past. This view of the Town Hall facing towards the castle is one of the most impressive of them.*

wealthy citizens of Cardiff to contribute towards the building costs. What they thought of that idea is indicated by the fact that it took six years to complete the work.

The design of the second Town Hall was very similar to that of the first. A flight of steps, flanked by attractive wrought-iron railings, led to the entrance of the council chamber. A prison and the shambles continued to occupy the ground floor, though there was one other addition. The southern end of the building was joined to a shop and the Shoulder of Mutton Inn.

Unlike the first Town Hall, the Georgian building is well illustrated. One fanciful picture of it can be seen outside Marks and Spencer's in the St David's Shopping Centre. Another attractive portrayal is the mural in the Golden Cross Hotel, which shows the building, with the statue of the Marquess of Bute in front of it, facing the castle in the 1850s. The Marquess died in 1848 and his statue was later moved to the southern end of St Mary Street. It now stands in Callaghan Square, south of the Central Station.

A painting of 1841 shows the walls of Cardiff Castle with the Town Hall standing prominently in High Street. To the west there is nothing but the river and open land. Another eight years would pass before the course of the Taff was altered and out of the old bed of the river would come Westgate Street and an enlarged Cardiff Arms Park.

The second Town Hall never seems to have been popular and increasingly became an impediment to traffic. Within 50 years there were complaints that the

*This well-known painting of 1841 shows the position of the Town Hall in High Street. In the distance the Cardiff Glass Works and the ships in the West Dock indicate Cardiff's growing industrial importance.*

building was lapsing into decay, but it continued to serve as the focus of local government well into the 19th century. It also staged major events from time to time in an age where few buildings were capable of fulfilling that role. John and Charles Wesley paid several visits to Cardiff in the 18th century, and in August 1788 John, making his last visit to the town, preached 'to the very greatest congregation' at the Town Hall.

In 1840 the Town Hall was acting as Cardiff' first fire station. Two fire engines were kept in the space below the building at an annual rent of 2s 6d. If there was a blaze the policeman on duty, aided by the general public, dragged the machines manually to the fire. Water was then drawn from the nearest available source, which could be the river, the canal, the wells or the public water pumps in High Street and Crockherbtown.

By this time it was clear that the Town Hall was inadequate to meet the needs of a growing borough. It was closed in 1853 but was not pulled down for another eight years. Part of the building was used as a storeroom for the uniforms and weapons of the Glamorgan militia, while the vestibule served as the Corn Exchange. Despite its inconvenient location, the Corporation tried to sell the building, but no offer was forthcoming, and its demolition in 1861 passed with few regrets. Nowadays, of course, such an historic building would probably be removed to the Museum of Welsh Life and rebuilt with loving care.

Cardiff's third Town Hall was erected on the west side of St Mary Street and extended as far back as Westgate Street. It is commemorated by a plaque on the wall of Hodge House in Guildhall Place. Public subscriptions paid for the cost of the two-storey building, designed in a Classical style with a Palladian frontage facing St Mary Street. At the time it was one of the few impressive buildings in Cardiff and, as open country lay to the west, a spectator on Leckwith Hill could see it clearly. When the third Town Hall was opened, there was confidence that it would serve the borough well beyond the 19th century.

However, within a few years, despite an extension that was added in 1880, the new building was under pressure as additional responsibilities were thrust on local government. Apart from these duties, the Town Hall provided accommodation for the Assizes and County courts, together with the headquarters of the police and fire brigade. The first fire station in Cardiff was built at the rear of the building in Westgate Street. Prestigious events were also held at the Town Hall, and in May 1856 Jenny Lind, 'the Swedish Nightingale', sang to an audience where the cheapest seat had cost 6s.

*The plaque of the third Town Hall was donated by Sir Julian Hodge in 1976. The architect was Horace Jones and it was built by W.P. James. The building was officially opened by John Batchelor on 1 June 1854.*

The third Town Hall is well illustrated. One of the murals in the Golden Cross reveals how it would have appeared in its Victorian heyday. One of many photographs captures the scene when the building was decorated with flags and bunting for the Coronation of Edward VII.

Outside the Town Hall was a drinking fountain. It was a gift from William Alexander, who in 1862 was Mayor of Cardiff. The fountain can still be seen in Kingsway, where it has been built into the wall near Greyfriars Road. The only item missing from the original monument is the drinking cup, presumably regarded as unhygienic in these health-conscious times. Another relic surviving from the third Town Hall is a sculptured monument, the theme of which is the 'Distressed Mother'. It was one of a pair modelled in marble by J. Evan Thomas, who also designed the statue of the second Marquess of Bute.

By the 1890s working conditions at the Town Hall were becoming increasingly difficult for the Corporation's ever-growing staff. The judges too were complaining about crowded conditions in the courts. There was agreement that a fourth Town Hall must be built, but there was no unanimity about where it should be sited. In what became known as 'the battle of the sites', the traders in St Mary Street saw no reason why the new building should not remain in its traditional location. Lascelles Carr, the editor of the *Western Mail*, favoured the Cardiff Arms Park as a site for the building. Apparently the sacred turf was not as hallowed at that time as it is now.

Another of the murals at the Golden Cross, portraying the Town Hall in the mid-Victorian period. The artist depicts a busy scene as horses, carts and pedestrians make their way along St Mary Street.

A young lad quenches his thirst at Alexander's Fountain. Originally a feature of the Town Hall, it was moved to the bridge of the Glamorganshire Canal at Mill Lane in 1908.

*When the canal bridge was demolished in 1952, the fountain was taken to Kingsway. There it remains to the present day, still an attractive monument but now minus the drinking cup.*

*The 'Distressed Mother' is an attractive sculpture rescued from the Town Hall prior to its demolition. It can be seen just inside the King Edward VII entrance of the City Hall.*

Another suggestion was to erect the Town Hall outside the Central Station in Temperance Town, an area which was regarded by many as dilapidated and rundown. Those who advocated this proposal argued how much better it would be for Cardiff's image if travellers coming out of the station were confronted with a fine civic building rather than an eyesore. In 1897 plans were drawn up to build the Town Hall on the site of the present bus station. Its advocates claimed that it

*This fine Gothic building might have been Cardiff's City Hall if those advocating the site in Temperance Town had won the day. It is an impressive setting but could not match that of Cathays Park.*

would be set in a magnificent square, 'big enough for 10,000 people to promenade'. Ornamental gardens would reach down to a riverside walk beside the Taff.

In the end, all these ideas came to naught. For many years the Corporation had cast covetous eyes on the open space in Cathays Park. The Marquess of Bute indicated that he was prepared to sell 59 acres of land in the park for the purpose of developing a new civic centre. The price was a reasonable £158,000, and the council had no hesitation in accepting this offer. On 23 October 1905, in what was to be the last important event at the Town Hall, Cardiff was proclaimed a city. When the new building was completed the following year, it became Cardiff's City Hall.

It was designed in a Classical style by the London firm of Lancaster, Stewart and Rickards, and its construction was entrusted to E. Turner and Sons. The firm has been responsible for many fine buildings in Cardiff, but none surpasses the City Hall, the cost of which was a mere £129,000. Magnificent shire horses dragged the heavy, white Portland stones from the docks to Cathays Park, where they were shaped with a special diamond saw. Nowadays, the council's headquarters is situated in Cardiff Bay, but the City Hall remains the venue for important events. Its Clock Tower can be seen from many parts of the city and harmonises with the dome over the council chamber. Few public rooms in Wales can match its Marble Hall, adorned with statues of Welsh heroes, or the Assembly Room where many famous events have taken place throughout the years.

*This postcard shows the fourth Town Hall in 1904 as it reached its final stages of completion. The following year Cardiff became a city and the Town Hall became the City Hall.*

*When the third Town Hall was pulled down, the Co-operative Wholesale Society built a warehouse on the site. One of the largest buildings in the city centre, it later became Hodge House.*

When the third Town Hall was demolished in 1913, the site passed into the hands of the Co-operative Wholesale Society. Guildhall Place was built to link St Mary Street with Westgate Street, and the Co-op built a warehouse which was completed by 1918. It remained there until the late 1960s when traffic congestion made it imperative to move elsewhere. For a few years the premises were used as government buildings until the property was acquired by Sir Julian Hodge as the head office of the Commercial Bank of Wales. Renamed Hodge House, the building is now occupied by two banks, a restaurant and a menswear shop. The opening of

*The Town Hall in 1913, the year before demolition began. It had been the seat of local government in Cardiff for over 50 years, but was unable to meet ever-increasing demands on its space by the 1890s.*

the City Hall had brought nearly 600 years of civic history to an end in High Street and St Mary Street. Now only the plaques remind us of the important roles these two streets once played in Cardiff's civic development.

**Further reading:**

**Rees, W.** *Cardiff, a History of the City*, Cardiff Corporation, 1969.

**Morgan, D.** *The Cardiff Story*, Dennis Morgan, 2001.

# Chapter 10
# A Famous Writer from Canton

A plaque to the memory of Robert Howard Spring can be seen at Barclays Bank on the corner of Albert Street, not far from where he was born on 10 February 1889. In those days Albert Street was known as Edward Street, and Henry and Mary Spring rented a couple of rooms at number 32. They had nine children, though only seven survived beyond childhood. The story of Howard's childhood is told in his fascinating book, *Heaven lies about us*. It is a moving tale of a boy's struggle against poverty and adversity in Cardiff at the beginning of the 20th century.

*In 1993 this plaque was placed on the wall of Barclays Bank in Cowbridge Road, not far from where Howard Spring was born. The portrait shows him in his later years after he became a successful writer.*

As their family grew, Howard's mother and father moved to a number of houses in Canton, one of which was in Harvey Street. The opening sentences of *Heaven lies about us* refer to 'Joe Andrew's Stone', where Howard and his friends used to meet. The stone was part of the Insole Hotel, where Joe Andrew was the publican. Since those days, the Insole has been rebuilt and Harvey Street is now a car park.

Howard never showed any bitterness about the plight of his family. He always maintained that you could be happy even if

*Albert Street, where Howard Spring lived for the first couple of years of his life. The photograph shows the street as it was in the 1960s, shortly before these houses were demolished.*

*Harvey Street, where, despite the shadow of poverty hanging over the Spring family, Howard had many happy memories. The house where he lived was the one with the lamp-post outside.*

you were poor, and he wrote with fondness of the antics and games he played with his friends. Local characters were brought to life, such as the man from the slaughter house in Market Road, 'an apparition from Hell... whose clothes and hands were always imbrued with blood'. Yet the same man showed his kindness by throwing a pig's bladder to the boys so that they could have a game of football.

Henry Spring was a jobbing gardener who was often out of work. With a large

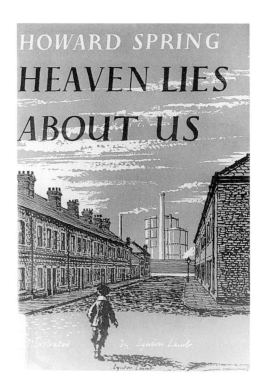

Heaven lies about us *was published in 1939 and is the story of Howard's childhood in Cardiff. It is written with humour, nostalgia and occasionally pathos. His observations make it a graphic account of life in Cardiff at the turn of the 20th century.*

family, an average wage of £1 a week meant that life was a constant battle to make ends meet. None of the family knew much about his background except that as a boy he had run away from his home in Cork. Henry rarely had any spare pennies, but if he did he would spend them on books purchased from a second-hand bookstall in Cardiff Market. On Sunday evenings there were reading sessions from *Pilgrim's Progress* or *Robinson Crusoe* around the fire, and if the children mispronounced a word more than once he would give them a clout. Howard's father died while he was still at school. His love of books was passed on to Howard, but he remembered his father as a dour, irritable man who rarely showed affection to his children: 'God rest his soul! He was a lonely and unhappy man'.

Howard always loved the countryside, which, in those days, was much closer to Cardiff than it is now. He wrote fondly of rambles to Castell Coch, Caerphilly and Leckwith Hill, accompanied by his elder brother, William. They enjoyed St Fagans Woods with its bluebells in spring, while Fairwater was another of their favourite excursions. 'In a stream at Fairwater, crossed by a railway bridge whose embankment was at times like a long snowdrift, so thickly the dog daisies grew there, we would fish by the hour'. With a bottle of water and a few slabs of bread and butter, the boys would gather blackberries or fish for tiddlers.

While Howard was still at school, he worked for 16 hours on Saturdays as an errand boy for a greengrocer in Canton. He loved the bustle of Custom House Street, Cardiff's Covent Garden, which was, 'wideawake, full of champing horses, and rattling harness, and shouting men'. Howard was paid 1s for his day's work, which did not end until 11pm, but he had no complaints as a 'sumptious' midday dinner was included. Later he incorporated his memories into *Tumbledown Dick*, a story for children.

All the older children were expected to contribute to the family budget. William won a scholarship to Howard Gardens Secondary School, but his parents could not afford to send him there. He had no choice but to look for work. Howard wrote movingly of how his mother 'scrubbed and charred' and took in washing to support the family after Henry's death. Though her life was hard, she never considered it a tragedy. She encouraged Howard in his reading and forecast that one day he would write books.

Howard left school at the age of 12. He had not enjoyed his schooldays at Severn Road, 'a gaunt and dismal barracks, full of stone stairs that echoed coldly

*Howard loved to fish in
the brook at Fairwater.
In* Heaven lies about
us *he wrote 'Fairwater
was easily to be got at
and in those days it was
as lovely as its name'.*

*A crowded scene at
Cory's Corner in
Butetown, 1900.
Spring found Tiger
Bay fascinating: 'It
was a dirty, smelly,
rotten and romantic
district, an offence and
an inspiration, and I
loved it'.*

to the clang of hobnailed boots'. Like most schools at that time, learning was by rote and discipline was harsh. Later he was to form a much happier relationship with one of his former teachers when he went to night school.

After a short spell as a butcher's lad, a job he hated, Howard became an office boy to an accountant at the docks. His wage was 4s a week, and, as he walked to work every day, he soaked up the atmosphere of Tiger Bay: 'A warren of seamen's boarding houses, dubious hotels, ships' chandlers smelling of rope and tarpaulin, shops full of hard ships' biscuits, dingy chemists' shops stored with doubtful looking pills, herbs, and the works of Aristotle'.

Howard attributed many of the important decisions in his life to chance and this particularly applied to jobs, when he was either 'pushed into them or lured into them'. The first time this occurred was when he asked his employer for an extra shilling a week. He was refused, so he gave in his notice and then had a stroke of luck. His sister was in domestic service with a sub-editor of the *South Wales Daily News*, and this connection led to Howard's employment as a messenger for the paper. William was already working as a secretary for its evening counterpart, the *South Wales Echo*. For nearly 40 years Howard Spring worked in the newspaper industry. He speculated that if he had been given the shilling and perhaps another half a crown a week a year later, he might have been satisfied and could have ended up as just another clerk in a docks office.

Howard loved his new job. This might involve running to the station to collect news from local correspondents or opening telegrams and sorting them into home news, foreign news and sports news before delivering them to the sub-editors. He soaked up the atmosphere of the machine room 'with the hot scent of fresh

*The offices of the* South Wales Daily News *and the* South Wales Echo, *where Howard began his newspaper career as a messenger, were situated along The Golate between St Mary Street and Westgate Street.*

newsprint'. Above all he enjoyed taking 'copy' from reporters, whether it was from a City Council meeting or, much more exciting, from the magistrate's court, 'listening with rapt attention to the charge against a girl for soliciting'.

Spring's next ambition was to become a reporter, and in those days this meant becoming an expert in shorthand. David Prosser, a future editor of the *Western Mail*, shared his determination and the two of them became close friends. Howard was also resolved to widen his education, and a trunkful of books left behind by a lodger was an incentive to make a start.

When William suggested they should both go to night school, a generous editor paid for their evening classes at the old university building in Newport Road. Five years of toil were to follow as Howard completed his education. By now he was a reporter, working 12 hours a day for six days a week. Evening classes and homework ate into his time for another three or four hours a day.

William, who always regretted being unable to accept the scholarship he had won, was never a strong lad. Despite his frail constitution, he 'drove at learning with a sustained frenzy'. His efforts were to kill him, and, while making a journey

*David Prosser, Howard and Anthony Davies, who later became night editor of the* News Chronicle. *David and Howard were great friends at the* South Wales Daily News *and both went on to follow successful careers.*

around the world in a cargo boat in an attempt to restore his health, he died at sea. Howard always looked on William as his greatest friend and was deeply saddened by the loss of his brother.

Finally, Howard matriculated and added to his 'library' by winning several prizes, which were presented at Cardiff's new City Hall. David Prosser recalled Spring's determination to learn French. So successful was he that within two years he won the Chamber of Commerce prize in that subject. The reward was a month's holiday in France, but as the winner had to follow a commercial career Howard sacrificed his prize. His future lay in writing and, as Prosser later recalled, 'Next to his beloved mother, the only thing that mattered was that novel he was going to write'. His first effort was returned by the publisher, so he attempted a short story, written for a boys' paper. He received a cheque for £1 12s 6d, the first that had ever come into the Spring household. Two more stories were accepted by the same paper, but as it went out of business, none of these early efforts were ever published.

In 1911 Howard left the *Echo* after one of his colleagues persuaded him to apply for a post on the *Yorkshire Observer*. It was the end of his life in Cardiff. As he left the city, 'the oppression of an irrevocable act overcame me… I had never had an adventurous spirit'. Soon after the outbreak of World War One he joined the *Manchester Guardian*. After first being rejected by the army on medical grounds, he later joined the Army Service Corps as a shorthand typist, working eventually at the British GHQ in France.

Returning to the *Guardian* after the war, Howard was sent to the London office in 1919 as a replacement for one of the staff who was ill. It was on this visit that he met Marion Ursula and for both of them it was love at first sight. Soon Howard and Marion were married and had two sons.

In 1931 Lord Beaverbrook invited him to work for the *Evening Standard*. Howard had reviewed books, both for the *Yorkshire Observer* and the *Guardian,* and now he followed in the footsteps of Arnold Bennett and J.B. Priestley as the book reviewer for the *Standard*. When the editor suggested an '*Evening Standard* Book of the Month', Howard's reputation and popularity soared in the literary world. When he left the paper in 1939 a colleague said, 'the *Evening Standard* lost its best descriptive writer and finest reviewer'.

*Two portraits of Spring as a young man at the beginning and end of World War One. The portrait of his mother reflects her 'indefatigable realism' that kept the family afloat. At the same time she encouraged him in his ambition to be a writer.*

Howard in 1914

Howard in 1918

Howard's mother

The urge to write had never left Howard. His first book, *Darkie & Co.*, was written for fun and was published for children in 1932, but it was his novels that were to make him world famous. Two remain classics and were made into films. *My Son! My Son,* a rather tragic story set in Cornwall, was a great success in Britain and America and was published in several different languages. Howard always said that he would not give up his newspaper career until he wrote a novel that sold 100,000 copies. *My Son! My Son* eventually sold more than a million and its success gave Spring his financial independence. *Fame is the Spur* was published in 1940. Believed by many to be based on the life of Ramsay Macdonald, it is the story of a Labour leader's rise and fall from humble beginnings.

During the 1930s Howard and Marion lived in London and bought themselves an attractive house at Pinner. Howard had always lived in large cities, but now he was looking for a more peaceful environment. During the excursions of his childhood, he had often imagined the country house or cottage that he would one day live in. Now, as he became a successful writer, he found it, not in South Wales but at Falmouth in Cornwall. First at St Mylor and later at the White Cottage, Howard was able to fulfil his childhood dream.

Spring had long been an admirer of Winston Churchill and this may have led to an unusual wartime adventure. When Churchill arranged to meet President Roosevelt for their first conference in August 1941, Howard was invited to join the party on board the *Prince of Wales.* Later he recalled the poignancy of sitting next to an emotional Churchill as they watched the film *Lady Hamilton* while the ship zig-zagged through the night to avoid marauding U-boats. A few months later Howard was shattered when he heard that the *Prince of Wales* had been sunk by the Japanese in the Indian Ocean.

Howard had never been strong, and his health began to deteriorate after the war. After one slight stroke, he recovered enough to write two more books, the last of which, *Wings of the Day*, was published in 1964. On 3 May 1965 another stroke brought about his death at the White Cottage in Falmouth, his home for the last 18 years. His ashes lie at St Mylor in Cornwall, the county he loved so much.

Though he later moved away from his native city, Howard Spring's attitude to life was shaped by those early years in Cardiff. David Prosser, his friend from those days at the *South Wales Echo*, was among those who testified to Howard's courage and belief in himself: 'Self pity was impossible for him'. He overcame all the handicaps of poverty and limited educational opportunities to become a

*The White Cottage in Pinner, the London residence of Howard and Marion. They were happy there, but in 1939 the family moved to Cornwall, where their last home was also named the 'White Cottage'.*

*Howard, seen here with H.V. Morton, on board the* Prince of Wales, *as it carried Winston Churchill to his first meeting with President Roosevelt. Spring was invited to accompany the Prime Minister as an observer of this historic event.*

*The shelves in Howard's study at the White Cottage in Falmouth were packed with books. The desk, which can be seen against the wall, was where he wrote all his novels.*

great writer. At the present time his work is no longer in fashion, but at the height of his career he was regarded as one of Britain's finest novelists.

**Further reading:**
**Spring, H.** *Heaven lies about us*, Constable, 1939.
**Spring, H.** *In the Meantime*, Constable, 1942.
**Spring, M.H.** *Howard*, Collins, 1967.

## Chapter 11
# Peerless Jim

The statue of Jim Driscoll is a tribute to a man who was probably the finest boxer that Wales ever produced and a person who was widely admired for his sportsmanship and great generosity. He was someone whom both the Welsh and the Irish residents of Cardiff were proud to acclaim and, 80 years after his death, his reputation remains untarnished.

Jim Driscoll was born in 1880 at 12 Ellen Street in the Newtown district of Cardiff. Newtown was an Irish enclave at that time, and Jim remained close to the community all his life. A year after he was born his father was killed after being hit by a railway engine, and his mother, Elizabeth, had to apply for parish relief. The Guardians of the Workhouse granted her 6s a week, which was later cut to 4s because, it was said, her four children looked too well fed and tidy. She added to this meagre income by selling fish in Newtown, and by working on the potato boats from Ireland at John England's Wharf on the West Dock. Later Elizabeth married Frank Franklyn, who was a labourer at the docks. Life was still far from easy as she had five more children by her second marriage, and Frank was sometimes unable to find work.

*Jim Driscoll's statue, silhouetted against the former AXA offices at the junction of Bute Street and Bute Terrace. The site is now being redeveloped as a hotel and, when completed, the statue will be given the prominence it deserves.*

*Elizabeth Driscoll, seen here with her private collection of Jim's trophies, was his proud mother. She faced a difficult time after the death of her husband until her second marriage to Frank Franklyn.*

Jim was 11 years old when he won his first fight. His older brother had been beaten up by the local bully, a big lad of 17. Despite his size, Jim sent him packing with a bloody nose and his love of boxing was born.

When he was 14, Driscoll worked for a time in the printing room at the *Western Mail,* where there was also a sports club. For a few years he fought as an amateur in competitions in Cardiff and the valleys. On one occasion, in a bare-knuckle

The portrait shows Jim in his prime, when those who fought him often found themselves chasing shadows. Around his waist is the Lonsdale Belt, one of the great trophies of British boxing.

contest at Leckwith Fair, he won a sovereign after staying on his feet for a minute against another lad, Badger O'Brien. They became close friends, and, as Jim's fame grew, Badger was usually a second in his corner.

His growing reputation brought him to the attention of Jack Scarrott, whose boxing booth toured throughout South Wales. For a sovereign a week, Jim fought up to a dozen times a day, often against much heavier opponents. By the time he was 18 he had fought more than 100 fights. In this harsh school, where he had to dispatch his opponent in three minutes or lose Scarrott a guinea, Driscoll perfected his skills as a boxer. Noting his ability to avoid punches, Scarrott hit on a new novelty. He offered a sovereign to anyone who could hit Jim on the nose within 60 seconds, while Jim stood still with his hands tied behind his back. He was only allowed to move his head, but such were his defensive skills that Scarrott's money was never in danger. Jimmy Butler wrote in the *News of the World* many years later: 'As a scientific boxer, Driscoll was incomparable. Everything he did in the ring was stamped with class'.

In 1901 Jim left the booths to turn professional. At first his success was limited to Wales, but in June 1906 he fought Joe Bowker for the British featherweight title at the National Sporting Club. This famous club was where the aristocracy donned evening dress and, after first dining at the Café Royal, took their seats for the evening's sport. Bouts were fought under the Marquess of Queensberry rules, and Lord Lonsdale ensured that these were properly observed. In a 20-round contest, Driscoll was trailing on points until the 17th round, when he knocked Bowker out with a blow that was so ferocious it jarred his elbow.

That same month Jim married Edie Wiltshire, whom he had been courting for more than 10 years. Her father was a wealthy publican and businessman who admired Driscoll as a boxer but was not happy about the idea of his daughter marrying him. However, love had its way and they were married at St David's Church in Charles Street.

In 1908 Jim was invited to tour America. Before leaving he promised to be back in time to participate in a charity show at the Park Hall in aid of Nazareth House. Coming from a staunch Catholic family, Nazareth House was Jim's favourite charity. The nuns, who provided care for orphan girls and elderly people, were popular among both Catholics and Protestants as they made no religious distinction when helping those in distress.

When Jim set foot on American soil the promoter, Jimmy Johnston, looked at his frail appearance and thought he was greeting a ghost. He soon changed his mind once he saw Driscoll in action, and in his two visits to the United States Jim was never defeated.

It was Bat Masterson, the US marshall from Dodge City, who gave Driscoll the nickname of 'Peerless', meaning that he had no equal. The tribute followed a

contest with Leach Cross, where the American barely landed a blow throughout the fight. Afterwards Leach called on Jim and, while he was asleep, gently landed his fist on the chin. 'There', he said, 'Don't let anyone say that Leach Cross never hung a glove on Jem Driscoll'.

Eventually Jim was matched with the world champion, Abe Atell. Before the fight, he caught a chill which turned to bronchitis. He was in bed until a couple of days before the contest, but he would not hear of attempts to delay it. Few gave Driscoll a chance as he weighed in for the contest, but, once the bell went, he made Atell look a novice. The *Daily Telegraph* reporter cabled home: 'Jim Driscoll left the ring unmarked. Atell's right eye was closed and his nose was all over his face... he is no longer the premier featherweight boxer in the world'. Whether Jim was officially the world champion was another question. It was the custom in those days for the newspapers to give the verdict if there was no knockout. Unanimously they proclaimed Driscoll the winner.

To put the matter beyond any doubt, the American promoter wanted a rematch. It would have brought Jim a small fortune, but to their astonishment he

*Nazareth House in North Road was one of several charities supported by Driscoll. In keeping his promise to appear at a charity event for the sisters, Jim gave up the chance to become official world champion.*

told them it would have to wait as he had promised to box for Nazareth House. They offered to send $1,000 to the charity, but Driscoll's response was, 'You make a promise, you keep it'. Though Jim returned to America in 1909, Atell was careful to avoid him and so, as far as the Americans were concerned, Driscoll was never officially the world champion.

Cardiff and the rest of Britain were certain that he was. Jim returned to a hero's welcome and a reception at Cardiff Castle in the presence of the Marquess of Bute and other dignitaries. Further success followed as he defended his British title three times to win the Lonsdale Belt outright. However, one bout was to prove too much for him.

In December 1910 Driscoll agreed to fight the world lightweight champion,

*The programme for the notorious fight between Driscoll and Freddie Welsh. The contest at the Roller Rink in Westgate Street was eagerly awaited between the rival factions in Cardiff and Pontypridd.*

Freddie Welsh from Pontypridd at the Roller Rink in Westgate Street. Welsh was at least eight pounds heavier and a superb if unscrupulous pugilist. He was notorious for his punching to the kidneys, but referee 'Peggy' Bettinson, sitting outside the ring, ignored Welsh's persistent fouling. As the fight turned into a street brawl, Jim became increasingly infuriated. After several blows to his kidneys and a head butt that almost broke his nose, a red mist descended on him. In the 10th round he went berserk and butted his opponent on the chin. Having ignored Welsh's fouls earlier, Bettinson now stopped the fight and awarded it to Welsh. Punches were thrown by the seconds and a riot broke out in the hall, which was eventually broken up by police armed with truncheons. Despite the provocation, Jim found it difficult to forgive himself as it was the only time in his life that he slipped from his own high standards of sportsmanship.

Driscoll retired in 1913 and was one of the first to enlist when the war began the following year. Initially he joined the Welsh Horse but soon became a sergeant-major in the Army Gymnastics Staff at Aldershot. Though his health was deteriorating, he fought more than 12,000 rounds in exhibition bouts and sparred with men about to be shipped off to the killing fields of Europe. For some, the last boast they ever made was the claim that they had sparred with the great Jim Driscoll.

After the war, though nearly 40 years old, Jim was persuaded to come out of retirement to help in the rebuilding of British boxing. Though his lungs were beginning to collapse and he suffered from boils and stomach ulcers, he agreed to fight Charles Ledoux, known as the 'Little Assassin'. Driscoll was ill in bed for four days before the fight, but in the first 15 rounds he gave the Frenchman a

boxing lesson. Then his strength drained away, and he was scarcely able to raise his hands. Ledoux, who was 12 years his junior, began hitting him at will and Jim's second, the ever-faithful Badger O'Brien, threw in the towel to save him from further punishment. It was a sad end to a distinguished career.

In that career Driscoll had earned a small fortune from boxing. He brought back nearly $4,000 from his first trip to America, but his problem was that he spent money as fast as it came in. One of his vices was gambling. Jim loved a flutter at Ely Racecourse and with his friend, Tim Driscoll, he opened a bookmaking business under the name of the 'Peerless Jim Agency'. After making excellent profits in its early days, the business sustained heavy losses in World War One. Jim lost much of his savings and Tim, almost everything.

Yet most of Jim's wealth disappeared because of his generous nature. He was a regular contributor to charities such as the Cardiff Infirmary, the Boots for Children Fund and of course Nazareth House. There were many who told him he was a fool when it came to money, including his wife, but Jim's answer was always the same, 'There's a lot of people in need, Edie'.

*Jim, partly kneeling, retaliated after enduring persistent fouling by Welsh and was disqualified by referee Bettinson after 10 rounds. The decision was followed by an outburst of violence among the crowd of 10,000.*

*The British Army boxing battalion entertained the troops with exhibition bouts. From left to right at the back stand Bombardier Billy Wells, Pat O'Keefe, Johnny Basham and Dick Smith. At the front are 'the mighty atom', Jimmy Wilde, Captain Bruce Logan and Jim Driscoll.*

*A photograph of Driscoll taken during a break from training at Ninian Park before his fight with Charles Ledoux. It is obvious from his haggard appearance that he was unfit to enter the ring.*

In Newtown people said 'No child went hungry and no family feared the landlord's knock as long as Driscoll had money'. Jack Roberts, a former opponent whom Jim had outclassed, ended his boxing career penniless. He always waited at the National Sporting Club for Jim to appear. Driscoll always gave him half a sovereign, which Jack promised to pay back. He never did and Jim would chuckle 'Poor old Jack. I have given him far more than I ever earned on the night I beat him'. Not long before he died, Driscoll said to an old sparring partner, Salam

*Ellen Street in
Newtown, shortly
before its demolition in
1966. Jim was born at
number 12, brought up
at number 3, and died
in the Duke of
Edinburgh Hotel on the
same street.*

*Few funerals in Cardiff
have matched that of
'Peerless Jim' on 3
February 1925. As the
coffin, draped with the
Union Flag, was placed
on a gun carriage,
100,000 people followed
the procession.*

125

*The grave of Jim Driscoll at Cathays Cemetery. The Sisters of Nazareth added to his headstone the title which he deserved but was never awarded, 'Retired featherweight champion of the world'.*

Sullivan, 'If only we could put the clock back, think of the money we could make today.' Salam replied 'What would be the use, Jim? You'd only give it away'.

A testimonial fund was opened for Driscoll on the same evening that he lost his last fight to Charles Ledoux. The fund eventually raised £5,000 and, as Jim's generosity was known to all, it was put in trust for him. In his last few years he kept the Duke of Edinburgh Hotel in Ellen Street, though Edie would not allow him to serve the drinks as he never charged the customers. He also reported fights for the *News of the World*, worked for Nazareth House and coached boys in boxing at the Central Athletic Club.

In December 1924 Jim caught a chill that turned to pneumonia. A month later on 30 January he died in the Duke of Edinburgh, aged just 44. A leading boxing magazine carried the headline 'The King is dead'. The funeral a few days later showed the enormous respect in which Driscoll was held. As Jimmy Butler later wrote, 'No other pugilist before or since has been mourned so greatly by his fellow men and women'. At one stage the procession was nearly two miles long. Peers of the realm, docksmen and businessmen mingled with boxers, miners and coal trimmers as the coffin was carried on a gun carriage. A guard of honour was provided by the Welsh Regiment and, after the Last Post, shots were fired over the grave. Children from Nazareth House, carrying wreaths, were in the procession, and later, at their own request, the Sisters of Nazareth paid for his headstone.

**Further reading**

**Cordell, A.** *Peerless Jim*, Coronet Books, 1986.

**Deakin, F.T.** *Peerless Jim Driscoll: the Original Welsh Wizard*, Crescendo Publications, 1987.

## Chapter 12
# Cardiff Markets

In 1991 a plaque was unveiled to commemorate the centenary of the Central Market. Throughout its history Cardiff has had several markets, though most of them were held in the open air until the 19th century. From the time of its earliest charters, the borough was given the right to hold a market twice a week on Wednesdays and Saturdays. When the clerk of the market rang his bell to indicate it was time for business to begin, High Street and the by-ways leading from it were crowded with visitors pouring into the town. They flooded in from the Vale of Glamorgan and the nearby villages and farms of Roath, Canton and Cathays, all of which would one day become suburbs of Cardiff.

The bustling excitement of market day is conveyed in Rowlandson's cartoon of 1797. The noise of horses, carts and all manner of livestock mingled with the voices of farmers, stall-holders and customers. Some bystanders, surrounded by curious children, were just keen to hear the latest gossip. The noisy atmosphere, though not the stench from livestock and rotting garbage, began to die away by midday as customers and traders started to disperse. For those needing refreshment before their homeward journey, there was a choice of 27 pubs in Cardiff, even though its population at that time was less than 2,000.

As late as 1790, there were only 25 retail shops in Cardiff and the market was essential, not only to buy food, but also to purchase such necessities as wool, cloth and crockery. Alderman John Winstone wrote an account of the High Street market as it was in the early 19th century, and his description suggests that it had changed little since the Middle Ages. Meat, vegetables and earthenware were sold in temporary stalls stretching from the Town Hall to the castle. Under the Town

*In 1991 the Central Market was 100 years old. To mark the occasion this plaque, placed on the stairs at the Trinity Street entrance, was unveiled by the Lord Mayor.*

THIS PLAQUE WAS UNVEILED BY
THE RIGHT HONOURABLE
THE LORD MAYOR OF CARDIFF
COUNCILLOR JOHN SMITH BSc (Econ).

IN THE PRESENCE OF
COUNCILLOR W. P. HERBERT,
CHAIRMAN OF THE LAND COMMITTEE,

ON 8TH MAY 1991 TO COMMEMORATE THE
CENTENARY OF THE CENTRAL MARKET

Hall there were two markets. One sold poultry, eggs, cheese and butter, while the other was reserved for the sale and grinding of corn.

At that time people baked their own bread, and unscrupulous traders tried to evade market tolls by buying large quantities of grain, which they then sold at an inflated price. As this practice caused hardship to the poor, a bye-law of 1708 ordered that the first two hours of trading at the Corn Market should be exclusively reserved for the needs of the townspeople. Only later, after the ringing of the bell, could 'higlers, badgers, bakers and all foreigners' make their purchases of grain.

An open-air market created problems of public health as animals were kept in pens or tied up in the street. In the 18th century attempts were made to separate livestock from the market used by the public. The Cattle Market was moved to Crockerton Street near the East Gate and the Pig Market was situated in St Mary Street between Quay Street and the Golate. An Act of 1774 gave street commissioners the power to order all stall holders to clear obstructions and rubbish after trading had ended for the day, but such regulations were not easily enforced.

As High Street and St Mary Street became much busier following the construction of the Glamorganshire Canal, the need to replace the open-air market with one under cover became obvious. The first attempt to provide such a facility

*Rowlandson's cartoon of Market Day in Cardiff shows the scene in High Street. It is sometimes disputed whether the setting is in fact Cardiff, as the Town Hall faces the wrong way. More likely this is artistic licence.*

was left to William Vachell, who owned a plot of land in High Street. His enterprise was a great success, although the Corporation insisted on collecting the traditional tolls set down in the borough charter. The popularity of Vachell's Market galvanised the council into building a covered market. When Vachell's Market closed, the site was used to build premises for the National Provincial Bank. It is one of Cardiff's few Georgian buildings and is now occupied by Crane's music shop.

The New Market, as it became known, was built in the garden alongside the County Gaol. Its architect was Edward Heycock, who had designed similar buildings at Shrewsbury and Dowlais. There is no doubt that he was conscientious in his work, as he was supervising the finishing touches to the building the night before the opening ceremony on 19 December 1835. The market, with its main entrance in St Mary Street, resembled a large shed about 200 feet long. Its façade was Georgian in style with three columns supporting a triangular gable. Entry was also possible through an arcade in Church Street, which remains there today. There may have been access from Trinity Street, though this is not clear from existing plans.

The New Market, which was lit by gas, was open daily apart from Sundays, Christmas Day and Good Friday. The Corn Market continued to be held at the old Town Hall until its demolition in 1861. As the population of Cardiff grew,

*Opposite page: The St Mary Street entrance to the New Market in April 1872. Both the market and the Borough Arms next door are decorated, the special occasion being the wedding of the Marquess and Marchioness of Bute.*

*This map of 1880 suggests a rather hemmed-in appearance to Cardiff's first covered market. Inside the narrow entrance from St Mary Street were the fish stalls, the opposite end to their position in the Central Market.*

*The two old cottages and the police headquarters stand to the left of Heycock's Market in this view of High Street in 1865. In the distance the house at the entrance to the castle was the High Corner House. It was pulled down in 1877.*

facilities to buy and sell animals were moved further away from the heart of the town, and in 1859 Market Road in Canton became the site for the Cattle Market.

Alongside the entrance to Heycock's Market were a pair of cottages. Next door to them were the Police Headquarters, where the County Gaol had stood until 1832. For over 300 years the gaol had been a fearful place where prisoners were never segregated and were often clapped in irons. Many of them never came to trial as they were carried off by smallpox or gaol fever. The gaoler, who purchased his office, made a living by extracting gratuities from the prisoners or their friends. Such payments were essential if their lives were to be made bearable. He did not always live on the premises and so escapes were not infrequent. In 1790 Judge George Hardinge, who regularly sat at the Assizes in Cardiff, demanded sweeping reforms. He advocated better conditions for prisoners and the appointment of a gaoler who would be resident on the premises and would be paid a salary in place of his 'perks'. These reforms appear obvious, but they were so slow in arriving that Hardinge threatened to move the Assizes from Cardiff to Cowbridge, while informing the King of the 'lamentable state' of the gaol. Even after these threats, it was nearly 10 years before the judge was satisfied with the state of the prison.

One of the last prisoners to be executed at the County Gaol, before a new prison was built in Adamsdown, was Richard Lewis, otherwise known as 'Dic Penderyn'. He had taken part in the Merthyr uprising of 1831 and was accused of wounding a dragoon while attempting to seize his musket and bayonet. Despite some very dubious evidence, Dic Penderyn was convicted and hanged on 13 August 1831. He became a martyr for working-class movements and was buried at Aberavon amid scenes of great emotion. A plaque to his memory was placed at the St Mary Street entrance to the market in 1980, and a ceremony to mark his martyrdom is usually held here on the anniversary of his execution.

As Cardiff became the largest borough in Wales, demands were made for a larger and more modern market. There were complaints that the existing building was poorly ventilated and it was described by one observer as 'the rankest compound of villainous smells that ever offended nostrils'. Various plans came to naught, among them a scheme put forward by Solomon Andrews, one of the leading businessmen in Cardiff. After his proposal was rejected, he decided to build on land he had acquired from the council, which included the two cottages and the police station next to the market. His Market Buildings had a frontage of 100 feet and were four-storeys high with a central tower. Within the tower was a camera obscura, offering splendid views of Cardiff from what was

*George Hardinge, the judge appointed to the Glamorgan circuit, was a colourful character, portrayed as the 'waggish Welsh Judge' in Byron's* Don Juan. *Fair-minded and normally a congenial companion, he was unrelenting in his pursuit for better conditions at the County Gaol.*

then one of the tallest buildings in the town.

Solomon's masterpiece was completed in June 1884, but a year later the Market Buildings were destroyed in one of the worst fires ever seen in Cardiff. Such was the intensity of the blaze that windows began to crack and paint began to peel from the doors of the Town Hall opposite. As the fire spread to the Borough Arms, only the courage and dedication of the fire brigade saved the market and Howell's store from the belching flames. Andrews showed his resolution

*The plaque of the County Gaol was donated by the National Union of Mineworkers. A ceremony marking the martyrdom of Dic Penderyn is usually held here every year on the anniversary of his execution.*

133

in adversity, and in 1886 the Market Buildings rose from the ashes, with a similar design except for the addition of a promenade on the roof. The *Pictorial World* praised the final result: 'For beauty, extent and adaptability, few buildings in South Wales... can compare with the superb pile erected by Messrs Andrews and Son'.

Four years later the foundation stone was laid for the Central Market. It was built on the site of Heycock's Market, which was now demolished, and a temporary wooden market was erected in The Hayes. The design of the new building was similar to its predecessor, though additional space increased its area by nearly 50 percent. The structure was mainly rectangular in shape and the St Mary Street entrance now passed through an archway under the Market Buildings. Originally the glass roof was painted every year to control the temperature inside the building, but later coloured glass was used for this purpose. At the centre of the hall was the market inspector's office with its attractive Clock Tower, which is still a feature of the building.

Stairs at each end led to a gallery which the council decreed should specialise in non-perishable items. The pet shops became a feature of interest, especially with children. At the Trinity Street entrance a triangular area was reserved for the fishmongers where Ashton's, who had a stall in the old market, became the principal tenant. The firm still occupies that site today. Another family business

*Undaunted, Andrews rebuilt on the ruins within a year. Given the title of 'Solomon's Temple' by some local wits, the Market Buildings still provide an imposing entrance to the Central Market, as this contemporary sketch reveals.*

*Built by Andrew Handyside of Derby, and supervised by William Harpur, the borough engineer, the Central Market is an excellent example of the use of wrought iron and glass in Victorian industrial architecture.*

*Fishmongers are increasingly difficult to find in Cardiff, which accounts for the popularity of Ashton's fish stall. Originally opening for business in 1866, Ashton's are the market's oldest tenants. This photograph was taken in 1923.*

which remained in the Market for more than 70 years was Roche's stall, which began by selling china in 1932. It later became a sandwich bar and continues to serve that purpose, though Mr Roche retired in 2004. Before becoming a household name, Marks & Spencer established one of their penny bazaars at the market in 1895. It was one of a number of such stalls that laid the foundations of a national institution.

When the building was completed at a cost of £16,000, the opening ceremony was performed by the Marchioness of Bute on 8 May 1891, a date marked at the Trinity Street entrance. The *Western Mail*, in reporting the event, commented that the market was 'a perfect model' and 'one of the best in the country'. For the small, specialist trader, the Central Market offered an alternative to the covered arcades of Cardiff, which tended to be more expensive because of their overheads. Originally the building remained open till late at night on Saturday, and after an evening on the town customers would visit the market to purchase food for their Sunday dinner. The best bargains were to be found near closing time when the prices on fresh produce were reduced.

Early in the 20th century the manager of the Central Market became responsible for other markets in the borough. A purpose-built wholesale fish market was opened on the site of St John's Infant School in The Hayes in February 1901. It was never a great success and, following heavy losses in the 1930s, it was closed in 1935. Underneath the building was a sub-station for the Cardiff Electricity Company and, when the fish market closed, the building became the showrooms for South Wales Electricity.

Despite the comfort of shopping under cover in inclement weather, people still have a yearning for the open-air markets of bygone days. Cardiff is no exception, and between 1915 and 1953 Hayes Island was a popular venue for fresh fruit and vegetables. As traffic increased and congestion became a problem, the fruit and vegetable market was moved, first to Mill Lane and then to Barrack Lane, where it still serves the people of Cardiff. In recent years local markets such as that at

*The market in the early 1900s. Among the stalls was Marks & Spencer's penny bazaar, opened by Michael Marks in 1895. It was only after World War One that the firm moved to their premises in Queen Street.*

137

A busy scene outside the
Trinity Street entrance
to the Central Market in
2005. The wrought-iron
grille, containing the
coat of arms of Cardiff,
was restored for the
centenary in 1991.

*A busy scene outside the Trinity Street entrance to the Central Market in 2005. The wrought-iron grille, containing the coat of arms of Cardiff, was restored for the centenary in 1991.*

Bessemer Road have become popular and provide opportunities for those seeking
a bargain.

As the market approached its centenary, the Council carried out a programme
of refurbishment and repair, though the building itself appears little different from

*This building, now occupied by Habitat, has been altered since it was the Fish Market on The Hayes. The two gables and the arched windows at the front have been removed and stone cladding now covers the walls.*

the time it was opened. It retains its Victorian character and, while many people have switched their allegiance to superstores, the Central Market in the heart of the city is still popular as it continues to offer a wide variety of products, some of which are not easily obtained elsewhere.

**Further reading:**

**James, B.L. & P. Riden** *Cardiff Central Market 1891–1991*, University College, Cardiff, 1991.

**Rees, W.** *Cardiff, A History of the City*, Cardiff Corporation, 1969.

# Chapter 13
# The Royal Infirmary

Before 1837 the principal source for medical treatment in Cardiff was the Glamorgan and Monmouthshire Dispensary at Mellard's Court near St John's Square. Its care was limited to those out-patients nominated by subscribers, who paid an annual fee of 10s 6d. Later the dispensary moved to larger premises in Union Street, but the service it offered became unable to meet demand as the population of Cardiff grew. By 1834 it was clear that the town needed something more than an out-patient service, and it was decided to build an infirmary on the site of a former leper hospital in Newport Road.

Daniel Jones, a wealthy lawyer from Beaupre, near Cowbridge, made a gift of £3,500, which was enough to pay for the building. The Marquess of Bute gave a further £1,000 and the 1834 Eisteddfod held in Cardiff contributed another £340. When the Glamorgan and Monmouthshire Infirmary and Dispensary opened its doors three years later, it had room for 33 in-patients. They were housed in an attractive building, rather like a manor house, with a fine portico and wrought-iron railings.

The infirmary was staffed by a full-time house surgeon, who was paid the modest salary of £100 a year, together with 'coal and candles supplied from the Institution'. His duties included visiting patients at home after their discharge from hospital and he was not allowed to receive any fees for private practice. A matron, whose salary was £20 a year, a nurse, a porter and a maid were the only other full-time staff. The house surgeon was required to co-ordinate the services of the honorary surgeons and doctors who visited the hospital regularly and gave their

services free of charge. One of matron's duties was to ensure that there was no improper use of alcohol in the hospital.

When the infirmary was opened, sanitation in Cardiff was deplorable and diseases such as smallpox, typhus and cholera were a regular occurrence. The hospital itself lacked running water and mains drainage for many years. The fear of hospitals was so great that many parents refused to allow their children to be vaccinated against smallpox. The infirmary performed its first operation in December 1837 when a boy's leg was amputated. It is recorded that he was, 'suffering most severely from the effects of a burn... We are happy to find the patient is going on well'. To prevent the spread of infection, people suffering from an infectious disease were denied admission, though they could receive treatment as out-patients. Also excluded were children under seven years of age, women who were pregnant and patients who were incurable or suffered from insanity or venereal diseases. Though this policy sometimes led to caustic remarks that only healthy people were admitted, the reality was that the hospital had to make the best use of its limited resources.

In 1859 the accommodation was increased to 52 beds and by 1873 a further expansion included a separate ward for contagious diseases. However, as the population of Cardiff continued to rise, the infirmary's management proposed an

*An engraving of the Glamorgan and Monmouthshire Infirmary in the early Victorian period. The University College of South Wales and Monmouthshire took over the building when the new infirmary was opened in 1883.*

increase in the number of beds to more than 100. Such a proposal was impossible to implement in the existing premises but it was another 10 years before a new infirmary was built.

In 1880 the Marquess of Bute offered four acres of land on Longcross Common as a site for a new hospital. The rent was a mere £15 a year and the £27,000 needed to build the second Glamorgan and Monmouthshire Infirmary was raised by public subscription. The hospital provided 100 beds when it was opened in 1883, though it was planned to double the number as funds became available. In its first year the infirmary treated 1,000 in-patients and 9,000 out-patients.

The former premises in Newport Road were leased to the new University College of South Wales and Monmouthshire. Later the university bought the building for £11,000 and, until the college in Cathays Park was opened in 1909, it was the focus of its activities. The building continued to be used until it was finally demolished in 1966. After World War One the Welsh School of Medicine was built next door to the original infirmary and medical students were trained there until the University Hospital was opened at The Heath.

As a voluntary hospital, the infirmary offered free in-patient and out-patient care to those who could not afford to pay for it. In its early days this principle was strictly upheld and people were either refused admission or discharged because they did not meet this criteria. To gain admission, other than in an emergency, a patient needed a letter, giving details of his financial circumstances, written by one of the subscribers to the infirmary. An ever-increasing debt eventually forced the Board of Management to make charges, and from 1911 patients paid 6d a day

*An engraving of the new Glamorgan and Monmouthshire Infirmary in 1883, soon after it was opened. The building has undergone many alterations since it was first designed in this Jacobean style by its architects, Seward and Thomas.*

towards the cost of their food. Out-patients were charged 3d for each visit, and 10 years later they were asked to make a payment according to their means.

By 1914 the infirmary was serving a population of nearly a million people in south-east Wales. Finances were given a much-needed lift as workmen in the mines and factories of the region were persuaded to donate 1d a week, later raised

*The Welsh National School of Medicine in the 1920s. The building was the gift of Sir William James Thomas and cost £90,000. Today the engineering department of the university occupies the site.*

*The Shand Ward for children in 1909. One of the original wards in the infirmary, it was named in honour of Frances Batty Shand, who was also renowned for her work with the blind.*

143

*The infirmary in 1910, just before it was renamed the King Edward VII Hospital. A memorial fund launched at this time helped to provide the finance for a new block of wards.*

*This painting by Margaret Lindsay Williams used to hang in one of the wards at the infirmary. Colonel Hepburn, accompanied by Matron Montgomery Wilson, talks to wounded soldiers from the Western Front.*

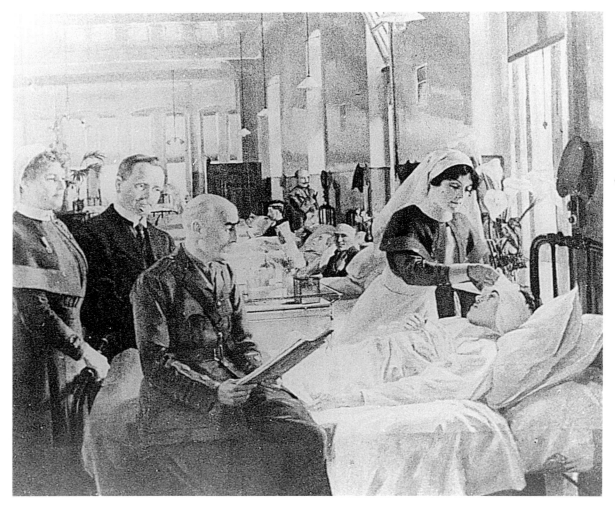

to 2d, in return for their treatment in times of need. This additional strain on resources did not always go down well with people in Cardiff, who regarded the infirmary as their own. They complained about 'derelicts from the hills' invading their hospital, especially when its name was changed to the Cardiff Infirmary in 1895. During the 1920s the hospital had a waiting list of over 1,000 people.

In World War One, the infirmary faced staffing difficulties as doctors and nurses left to serve in the forces. Colonel Hepburn, Commanding Officer for the 3rd General Western Hospital, was provided with 100 beds for wounded soldiers. The number soon proved to be woefully inadequate to deal with the casualties of that dreadful bloodbath, and five schools in Cardiff were converted into hospitals.

Over a period of time, new wards and operating theatres, together with other facilities such as an X-ray department and a nurses' home in Newport Road, were added to the infirmary. The beautiful chapel on the corner of Newport Road was a gift from Mrs John Nixon and was opened in 1921. Houses in Glossop Terrace were purchased to provide a maternity hospital, though, as it lacked an operating theatre, patients requiring caesarean operations were wheeled across the road on a trolley. Not until after World War Two was a fine new maternity hospital built on the site. As the infirmary grew to meet its growing demands, the original four-acre site became six. Every available corner was filled and the limited space within a built-up area ensured that the complex began to resemble a maze.

The medical hierarchy was similar to that of the earlier infirmary. Visiting doctors and surgeons continued to give a free service, but as the hospital expanded in size the resident staff increased. By 1914 there were three house surgeons who were paid £60 a year. In 1914 they threatened to resign unless their salary was

*The Royal Infirmary in the 1950s, showing the balconies which were erected outside many wards earlier in the century. The balconies were later enclosed to provide more accommodation in the wards.*

increased to £100 and the shortage of medical staff at the outbreak of war ensured that their demands were met.

As a charity, the hospital was completely dependent on public generosity. Wards were named after wealthy benefactors such as Bute, Tredegar, Windsor, Radcliffe, Cory and many others. For £1,000 individuals and organisations could endow a bed in perpetuity, together with the privilege of recommending the patient who should occupy it. A plate above each bed named these donors, among them such groups as the Whitchurch Golf Club, the Meat Traders or the Municipal Bowlers. Smaller donations also brought privileges. An annual payment of two guineas allowed the subscriber to nominate one in-patient and 10 out-patients to the hospital during a year.

*Every gift made to the infirmary was publicly acknowledged in some form or other. This is one of the many tablets and plaques at the hospital, remembering those who contributed to its work before the arrival of the National Health Service.*

Fundraising came from a variety of sources. There was an annual flag day and churches donated their collections on Infirmary Sunday, held every April. School children offered their pennies and the Lady Aberdare League gave a brooch or medal to children who collected money for the hospital. Celebrities offered their services to provide much-needed cash injections. The famous soprano, Dame Adelina Patti, sang at charity concerts, and Lord Lonsdale organised a sporting week in the borough with boxing matches and other events. The council made a donation of £1,500 a year, which was later increased to £2,000.

The efforts of rich and poor show Victorian charity at its most generous. Nevertheless the expenditure of the infirmary always exceeded its income, a familiar tale in today's National Health Service. While the sums of money given to the hospital were considerable, so were the demands made on it. When new wards

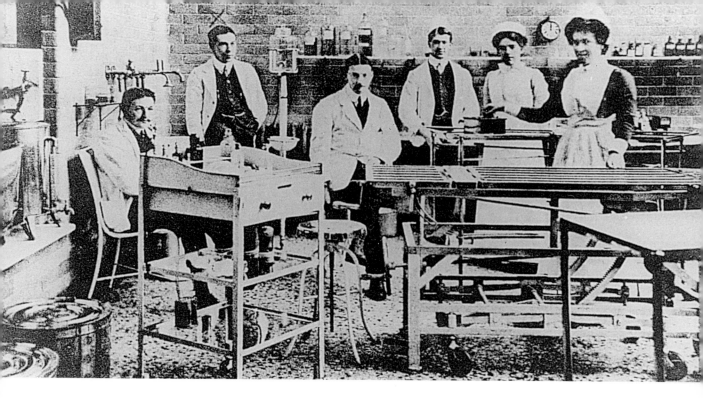

were added in 1895 it was a further six years before they could receive patients due to a lack of funds. Wards were lit by gas until 1903, when the Marquess of Bute paid for the cost of installing electric lighting throughout the building. Previously it was only available in the main operating theatre.

For many years the overdraft of the infirmary was personally guaranteed by the Honorary Treasurer, Lord Aberdare. In 1920 the debt rose to £50,000, and he felt he could no longer accept such a responsibility. The Management Committee decided to relieve him of the burden by petitioning for a royal charter. The infirmary had been renamed the King Edward VII Hospital in 1911 following the death of the King, but after receiving its charter in 1923 it became the Cardiff Royal Infirmary. Its finances continued to be under pressure despite a grant from the Voluntary Hospitals Association, a body set up by the government to help charity hospitals.

In World War Two the infirmary itself came under attack. During an air raid in September 1940 over 100 windows were broken and, when a 500lb bomb hit a house in Longcross Street, a major disaster was only averted as it failed to explode. The raid of 2 January 1941 tested the resources of the infirmary to the full as it cared for those who had suffered wounds during the attack.

Some of them were still in the infirmary on 3 March when it suffered its greatest ordeal of the war. That night a bomb struck the nurses' hostel in Newport Road, though luckily the nurses were all on duty. While a surgeon was operating in one of the theatres, a large window was blown across the room and the lighting failed. A nurse held the torch as he continued to operate in an adjoining room. Incendiaries fell on the chapel, the decontamination unit and a store containing

*The medical staff in the original operating theatre at the infirmary. Their equipment appears rather archaic by today's standards, but until 1903 this was the only room in the hospital to have electric lighting.*

inflammable substances. Fortunately help was close at hand as the fire brigade occupied a sub-station in the basement of the partially-built maternity hospital in Glossop Terrace. Amazingly there were no serious injuries, but several wards were so damaged that they did not reopen until after the war and patients were evacuated to other hospitals. Normal service ceased for a time, though the infirmary continued to function as a casualty clearing station. On 14 April the Prime Minister and Mrs Churchill visited the infirmary to compliment the staff on their devotion to duty and to offer sympathy to those injured in the Blitz.

On 6 July 1948 the National Health Service brought to an end the contribution

*The splendid
architecture of the
Royal Infirmary stands
out in this photograph
of the Royal Infirmary
in 1977. However, its
Victorian grandeur
could not hide its
problems as the hospital
tried to keep pace with
the growing demands of
modern medicine.*

that voluntary hospitals had made to the health of the nation. As a part of the new regime the Royal Infirmary served the people of Cardiff and South Wales for another 50 years. At its peak in the 1930s the hospital had contained 500 patients. Since that time numbers had fallen but conditions remained so overcrowded that a new hospital was essential. The University Hospital of Wales was opened in 1971, but the infirmary continued to play a valuable role in treating the sick until its closure in March 1999.

Since then a passionate campaign has been waged to keep the Cardiff Royal Infirmary open. The existing building is regarded as a fire risk and cannot be reopened as a hospital. Some National Health services are still provided at the infirmary, but promises to provide a community hospital on the site have so far not been met. The infirmary was described by Arnold Aldis, Dean of the Medical School, as 'a friendly, homely hospital' where 'the atmosphere was more that of a family than an institution'. Many share his affection for the 'Royal', among them a former nurse: 'In Cardiff, the infirmary is the people's hospital and we will keep fighting until someone listens to us.'

**Further reading:**
Aldis, A.S. *Cardiff Royal Infirmary 1883–1983,* University of Wales Press, 1984.

## Chapter 14
# Memories of a Century of Conflict

The wars of the 20th century, involving British people all over the world, are remembered with numerous plaques and monuments in Cardiff, particularly in Cathays Park. Many of them are a tribute to the Welshmen who fought in these campaigns, but others are a reminder of the suffering felt by the civilian population of Cardiff in World War Two.

The earliest of these monuments is the Boer War Memorial in Cathays Park. Originally erected outside the City Hall, it was moved a few yards away in 1974 to make way for the Boulevard de Nantes. The monument is dedicated 'to the memory of the Welshmen who fell in South Africa 1899–1902'. On it are the names of 878 men who died in the Boer War. Most of them were attached to the various Welsh regiments, but men from 102 other units, in which Welshmen served, are also recorded on the memorial. In addition, two nursing sisters, who gave their lives caring for the wounded, are named on the monument.

The *Western Mail* took the lead in raising subscriptions to pay for the memorial, designed by Alfred Toft. It was unveiled on 20 November 1909 by General Sir John French. More than 60,000 people were present in Cathays Park to see the ceremony and in his speech French said 'There are no regiments that have seen harder fighting or have been more constantly engaged in upholding the honour and glory of the Army and Empire than the regiments of the Principality'.

The first contingent of the Royal Welsh Fusiliers arrived at Durban in November 1899. There were only 850 of them initially, but it was not long before their ranks were swollen by more Welsh troops. They were soon in action, attacking the Boers across the River Modder in an attempt to relieve the garrison at Ladysmith. In that action alone, 19 men were killed, but by March 1900 the siege had been lifted. In his speech at the unveiling of the monument, the Lord Mayor of Cardiff recalled how the volunteer reservists set out for South Africa from the

*The names of the Welshmen who died in the Boer War are engraved on this memorial. It is made from white Portland stone with two bronzed figures. One denotes warlike courage, the other the grief of battle. Above them is the winged Angel of Peace.*

iron works, the mines and the railways of South Wales. These territorials included the Third Battalion of the Welsh Regiment, drawn from the Glamorganshire Militia, described by the press as, 'a fine body of men, most of whom are miners'. After entrusting their colours to the Mayor for safe keeping, they arrived at Capetown on 1 March 1900. More than 30 men from the Third Battalion were killed in action or died from disease during the two years they spent on the veldt. Their names are inscribed on the memorial in Cathays Park and on a commemorative tablet at Llandaff Cathedral.

*The Third Battalion of the Welsh Regiment spent two years in South Africa and sustained heavy casualties. This plaque in Llandaff Cathedral is dedicated to the memory of those who died.*

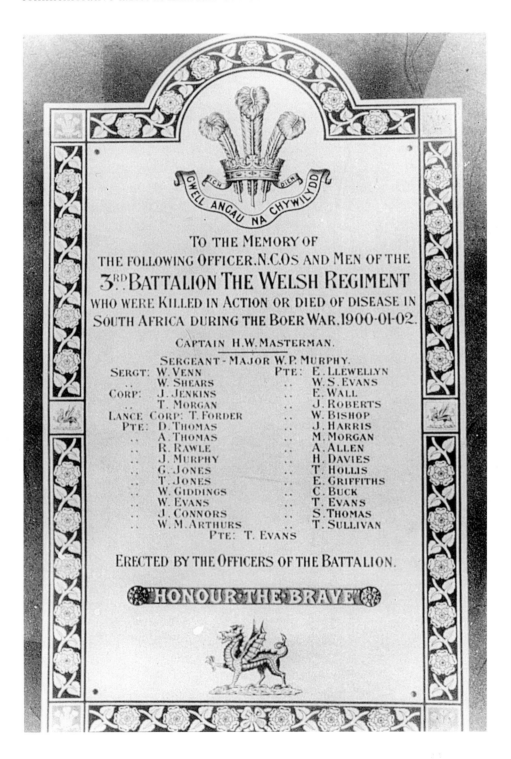

The Third Battalion returned to Cardiff in March 1902, led by 'De Wet', a stubborn goat they had captured from the Boers. Their colours were ceremoniously returned to them by the Mayor at Cardiff Arms Park. They then marched proudly through the town amid jubilant crowds, while the bands played *Men of Harlech*, *Tommy Atkins* and *Red, White and Blue*. As the battalion made its way to Maindy Barracks, military discipline broke down as friends and relatives joined the ranks of marching men. At Maindy the troops were discharged after being given £1 of their back pay, the rest wisely having been sent to their homes. As the war finally came to an end, there were similar scenes throughout Britain. It was a time of imperial pride with the British Empire at its zenith, though a strong body of opinion in the country, led by Lloyd George, was opposed to the war.

The casualty list was a foretaste of what was to come as the 20th century made its grim progress. The outbreak of war with Germany in 1914 led to a burst of enthusiastic patriotism. People from all walks of life rushed to answer Kitchener's cry, 'Your King and Country need you', and two battalions were formed in Cardiff.

The Cardiff Commercial Battalion embraced people from all walks of life, many of them colleagues and friends in the same workplace or football team. They

*The crowds cheer, the band plays patriotic tunes and the flags are out as Welsh troops, home from South Africa, march along Queen Street on their way to Maindy Barracks in 1902.*

were better known as the Cardiff Pals and began their training at Maindy Barracks. Their first taste of action was in France, but in November 1915 they were despatched to Salonika, where they faced the Bulgarians led by German officers. The enemy were tough opponents who inflicted heavy casualties on the Pals, though many were to die from malaria and other diseases. Their commander, Lieutenant-Colonel H.J. Wingate, later wrote 'No troops could have behaved with greater gallantry, and the operation will add another chapter to the glorious history of the Welsh Regiment of which the Pals were a very important part'.

Lieutenant-Colonel Frank Gaskell, whose father was chairman of Hancock's Brewery, was an officer in the Boer War. On the outbreak of hostilities in 1914 he played an important part in raising the 16th City of Cardiff Battalion, which incorporated the City's coat of arms in its badge. Gaskell never lacked courage. He was shot in the jaw in the early months of the war and was invalided home. When he returned to active service, he broke his leg in a riding accident. Once again he returned to France only to suffer a mortal wound at Merville, when a bullet struck his ammunition pouch in May 1916. He was buried in the military cemetery at Merville, and in Cardiff there are two memorials to his bravery.

The battalion itself took part in some of the worst fighting of the war. Two months after Gaskell's death, the City Battalion joined other men of the Welsh Regiment in the Battle of the Somme. At Mametz Wood in Picardy a memorial depicting a red dragon pays tribute to all the men of Wales who fought there. The

*The plaque at St John's Church in the centre of Cardiff pays tribute to Lieutenant-Colonel Frank Gaskell, who was killed in May 1916. There is a similar memorial at St Isan's Church in Llanishen.*

IN LOVING MEMORY OF
LIEUT. COLONEL FRANK HILL GASKELL,
OF THIS CITY.

IN THE GREAT WAR HE RAISED AND
COMMANDED THE 16ᵀᴴ (CARDIFF CITY)
BATTALION, THE WELCH REGIMENT;
HE WAS TWICE SEVERELY WOUNDED,
AND DIED OF WOUNDS AT
MERVILLE, FRANCE, MAY 17ᵀᴴ 1916,
AGED 37 YEARS.
"WHO HAD IT NOT IN HIM TO FEAR."

City Battalion, together with the South Wales Borderers and the Welsh Fusiliers, mounted an assault to take Mametz Wood on 7 July 1916. The wood, less than half a square mile, was finally taken four days later. On that first day alone, withering machine gun fire cut down 600 Welshmen, 137 of them from the battalion. Later those who had survived were to undergo a further martyrdom at Passchendaele.

When the bloodletting finally ceased on 11 November 1918, there was an outpouring of relief. Hooters and sirens signalled the end of hostilities and huge crowds gathered in St Mary Street and Queen Street to celebrate the dawn of peace. Amid the joy of victory, there was a recognition of the enormous sacrifice that had been made to achieve it. There was also a determination, alas unfulfilled, that this was 'a war to end wars'.

The dead of World War One are honoured with war memorials in nearly every parish of the United Kingdom, but in July 1917 Councillor Herbert Thompson proposed that a National War Memorial should be erected to the Welshmen who had perished in that dreadful conflict. Two years later the *Western Mail* opened a fund to place a monument in Cathays Park to the 35,000 soldiers from Wales who had fallen in the service of their country. More than £25,000 was raised but it was nearly 10 years before the memorial saw the light of day.

The original commission for the work was given to Sir Thomas Brock, but his

*St Mary Street on 11 November 1918. Joyful faces greet the dawn of peace, but the celebrations on Armistice Day were muted for those who had lost loved ones in this terrible conflict.*

design proved too expensive. While he was working on a new design he died, and the monument was finally completed by J. Ninian Compter. Initially, it was intended to erect it on the circular green outside the City Hall. Both the city council and the hierarchy of the National Museum of Wales objected to the site on the grounds that it would spoil the spacious, uncluttered appearance of these two fine buildings. Another proposal to place the memorial in the Friary Gardens was rejected by Lord Bute, who refused to allow the erection of a monument near the statue of his father. Not until August 1925 was it finally decided that the War Memorial should be set in Queen Alexandra Gardens. One wonders why there was so much debate, as a more beautiful and peaceful site would be hard to imagine.

A year later, work at last began on the construction of the cenotaph, and it was unveiled by the Prince of Wales on 12 June 1928. He paid tribute to the sons and daughters of Wales 'who, at the stern call of duty, streamed forth from city and remote village… to give their lives for the land they loved'. Representatives from the British Legion and former prisoners of war were present at the ceremony. The *Western Mail*, which devoted considerable coverage to the ceremony, believed the

*The Welsh National War Memorial is superimposed on the Friary Gardens in this photograph of Cathays Park in the 1920s. It was one of the suggested sites for the memorial, but wisely it was eventually erected in Queen Alexandra Gardens.*

monument should be 'a reminder … not only of the glory of war, but also of its folly'.

The circular Corinthian columns of the cenotaph enclose a sunken court with a fountain standing in its centre. Entry to the monument is through three porches, each of which leads to the figures of a sailor, an airman and a soldier. All of them hold up a wreath towards the winged Messenger of Victory who holds a sword in the form of a cross. Beneath the messenger, inscribed in Latin, are words meaning, 'In this sign shalt thou conquer'. Inside the colonnade is an inscription from Sir Henry Newbolt: 'Remember here in peace those who in tumult of war by sea, on land, in air, for us and for our victory, endureth unto death'. On the outside of the memorial is an epitaph in Welsh: 'I Feibion Cymrua roddes eu Bywyd dros ei

*The beautiful setting for the Welsh National War Memorial. It was designed by J. Ninian Compter and its construction was carried out by E. Turner and Sons, another fine example of their craftsmanship.*

Gwlad yn Rhyfel. MCMXIV–MCMXVIII'. The translation reads, 'To the sons of Wales who gave their lives for their country in the war of 1914–1918'.

The names of those Welshmen and women who died in World War One were also recorded in illuminated script by Graely Hewitt in an attractive leather book. During the unveiling ceremony, Britain's great wartime leader David Lloyd George presented the book for safe-keeping to Lord Aberdare, President of the National Museum of Wales. Later it was deposited in the Temple of Peace, where it can be seen on request.

In his address, the chairman of the organising committee, G.F. Forsdike, commented, 'We hope that there may grow such a hatred of war, that those who succeed us may say… war has indeed vanished from the earth'. World War One is still remembered as the Great War, and in 1938 King George VI, during the royal visit to Cardiff, paid homage at the memorial as his brother had done 10 years earlier. Yet already the storm clouds were gathering and another terrible clash of arms was little more than a year away. There were those who claimed it had already begun.

When the Spanish Civil War broke out, 174 volunteers from South Wales, many of them miners, joined the International Brigade to fight for the Republican cause against Franco. Their memorial in Alexandra Gardens, displaying the olive

*George VI lays a wreath at the memorial in 1938. Nearly 20 years had elapsed since the end of World War One, but already the prospect of another, even more terrible, conflict was casting its shadow.*

tree of peace, is 'dedicated to the Welsh Volunteers for Liberty who defended democracy in the Spanish Civil War 1936–38'.

Harry Dobson was a typical volunteer. When he was arrested after a battle with Moseley's Blackshirts in Tonypandy, he made his way to Spain and was killed at the Battle of the Ebro in July 1938. In all, 21 of the Welsh volunteers paid with their lives. Morien Morgan was an idealistic student from Cardiff who travelled through France to join the International Brigade. After a minimum of training he was captured by Franco's forces. Earlier in the war, prisoners had been shot by the Fascists but, as they were on the verge of victory, Morien was released in January 1939. Other sympathisers ran the Fascist blockade to bring food and supplies to the beleaguered Republicans. They also smuggled out more than 1,000 refugees, many of them children, and the Cardiff Committee for Spanish Relief established a home for 50 Basque children at Caerleon.

The Spanish Civil War is often regarded as the dress rehearsal for World War Two, a people's war as no previous conflict had been. Civilians, both men and women, had played a prominent role in World War One, but they never faced danger on the scale that now rained down from the sky. The worst air raid against Cardiff took place on 2 January 1941. In the first hour of the attack, 60 people were killed in Riverside, and Llandaff Cathedral was severely damaged after being struck by a landmine. Following the raid, many of the victims were buried in a mass grave at Cathays Cemetery. In its report, the *South Wales Echo* commented 'High and low, young and old, mingled around the communal graves… it was a scene that those who witnessed it will never forget.'

A plaque in Corporation Road recalls the most terrible single incident of that night. The cellar of Hollyman's Bakery had been reinforced as an air-raid shelter and, when the bombs began to fall, 32 people trooped into the cellar. When it was struck by a high explosive bomb, all those in the shelter were killed. Wardens brought out as many bodies as they could before filling in the crater, but beneath Clarence Hardware Store lie the remains of the deceased whose bodies were never recovered.

The Blitz affected every part of the city and another tragedy occurred on 29 April in Cathays. That night two landmines fell on Llanbleddian Gardens and Wyverne Road, killing 23 people. Among them were

*The Welsh contingent of the International Brigade that fought against Franco in the Spanish Civil War is remembered in this simple stone monument. It was unveiled by Michael Foot on 27 October 1992.*

*Some of the victims of the Blitz were buried at Cathays Cemetery on 8 January 1941. The Bishop of Llandaff led the service and the Lord Mayor, wearing black crepe on his chain of office, was among the mourners.*

IN MEMORY OF
THOSE WHO DIED
DURING THE BLITZ
2ND JANUARY 1941
AT
HOLLYMANS BAKERY
ERECTED BY GRANGETOWN LOCAL HISTORY SOCIETY

*The Grangetown Local History Society dedicated this plaque to the memory of the 32 people who were killed while sheltering in the cellar of Hollyman's Bakery on 2 January 1941.*

the 10 members of the Palmer family, whose Anderson shelter was no protection against a direct hit. Just before the 50th anniversary of VE Day, a memorial was placed in Cathays Cemetery near the graves of war victims. The Palmers are among the names inscribed on it, reminding future generations that this was a war where civilians faced similar dangers to those fighting in the armed services. In all, 355 people in Cardiff died in the air raids of World War Two and 502 were seriously injured.

Another reminder of World War Two is the monument in Cardiff Bay, recalling the heroism of merchant seamen from Wales who fought in the Battle of the Atlantic. They ensured that Britain received the food and vital supplies it needed to carry on the struggle against Nazi Germany. The memorial depicts a timeless face and a beached ship's hull on its side. In all, 30,000 merchant seamen died in facing the onslaught from the U-boats, and the mosaic surrounding the monument pays its tribute to those who came from Cardiff, Barry and Penarth.

Even after a ship was torpedoed, the survivors faced further horrors adrift in the Atlantic. Emil John from Barry was on the *Athel Knight* when it was sunk by a U-boat in May 1942. He found himself in an open boat with 26 of the crew who had escaped from their stricken vessel. While they drifted for a month, some of them died from wounds or exposure before they reached safety at St Bartholomew

*Clarence Hardware now stands on the site of that horrific tragedy. The plaque can be seen above the name of the shop in Corporation Road. The bones of some of the victims lie beneath the foundations of the building.*

The landmine was a terrifying weapon which wreaked slaughter when it fell on a built-up area. This was Wyverne Road, where the Palmer family was wiped out during the raid of 29 April 1941.

The memorial to those who died in the Cardiff Blitz was unveiled on 6 May 1995 in Cathays Cemetery. The ceremony was led by the Lord Mayor, Ricky Ormonde, and among those present were many who had lost relatives in the bombing.

THIS MEMORIAL COMMEMORATES THOSE WHO LOST THEIR LIVES DURING THE CARDIFF BLITZ IN 1941 AND WHO ARE BURIED HERE. UNVEILED BY THE RT. HON. THE LORD MAYOR OF CARDIFF COUNCILLOR D. RICKY ORMONDE ON 6TH MAY 1995

DONATED BY Mossfords

in the West Indies. During that time, Emil lived on a couple of squares of chocolate a day, a little Horlicks and a tiny ration of pemmican, a kind of dried meat. In searing heat, his water ration was less than half a pint a day.

In St John's Church, the Burma Star window reminds us of those Welshmen who served in that cruel and bitter war against the Japanese in south-east Asia. The window depicts a typical Burmese background. Overlooking it is the Burma Star, awarded to all who fought in the campaign, together with the badges of the Army, Navy, RAF and Merchant Navy. Those who fought in Burma endured the impenetrable undergrowth of the jungle, vicious mosquitos, oppressive sticky heat and, in the monsoon season, torrential rain, which turned the jungle into a quagmire. Animal tracks were often the only roads and, as these were also used by the Japanese, a sudden battle could erupt at any time. Though the 14th Army under Field-Marshal Bill Slim was sometimes nicknamed the 'Forgotten Army', they showed their courage in overcoming a ruthless foe.

One group of Welsh soldiers who suffered appalling cruelty at the hands of the Japanese were men from the 77th Heavy Artillery Battalion. Similar to the pals battalions of World War One, the 77th was raised in Cardiff and contained many famous Welsh sportsmen. Among them were Les Spence and Wilfred Wooller, both Welsh rugby internationals, and Ernie Curtis who had played in Cardiff

*After a two-year campaign by the Merchant Navy Memorial Committee, the Merchant Seafarers' War Memorial was unveiled in 1996. The inscription reads 'In memory of the merchant seafarers who died in time of war'. The sculptor, Brian Fell, was himself the son of a merchant seaman.*

163

*The Burma Star window in St John's Church. The epitaph echoes the famous words of the Siege of Kohima, the turning point of the Burma campaign: 'When you go home tell them of us and say, for your tomorrow we gave our today'.*

*Opposite page: 'To save one life is as if you have saved the world'. Raoul Wallenberg is remembered in this simple monument, unveiled in Queen Alexandra Gardens by the Swedish Ambassador on 24 November 1985.*

City's Cup-winning team. The battalion was captured when the island of Java fell to the Japanese in 1942. Only one in five of the original contingent returned to Wales three years later. Some perished in the infamous Changi Prison, while others were worked to death either in Japan or on the notorious Burma-Siam Railway. As people greeted the end of the war with relief on VJ Day, many families wondered whether their husbands, brothers or sons had survived the brutal treatment meted out to them by the Japanese.

*As the crowd gathered in Cathays Park on VJ Day, the* South Wales Echo *carried the headline, 'The World at Peace', but there was anxiety about the fate of prisoners of war still in Japanese hands.*

A memorial in Queen Alexandra Gardens is dedicated to the life and work of Raoul Wallenberg. In 1944 he was Secretary of the Swedish Legation in Budapest, and during his six-month stay in the city he saved the lives of 100,000 Jews by providing them with Swedish passports. Wallenberg disappeared after the war and was executed by the KGB in 1947 after the Russians accused him of spying for the Americans and the British. He was officially named a 'Righteous Gentile' by the state of Israel and was given honorary citizenship by the United States and Canada. The Cardiff Raoul Wallenberg Committee, one of a number throughout

the world, was formed after an exhibition about his life at St David's Hall in 1983. It was this committee that erected the monument as 'a token to his great humanity'.

In Alexandra Gardens, set in a little secluded clearing surrounded by cedar trees from the South Atlantic, a granite stone is dedicated to the six men from Cardiff who died in the Falklands Campaign of 1982. A Celtic cross on the Falkland Islands also honours their memory.

One of those who died was Terry Perkins from Cathays, a marine engineer

*The memorial stone to the soldiers from Cardiff who gave their lives in helping to liberate the Falkland Islands. It was unveiled on 24 October 1983 by the Lord Mayor, Mrs Olwen Watkin, in the presence of the bereaved families.*

mechanic serving on HMS *Glamorgan*. The other names on the memorial were victims of the tragedy at Bluff Cove in which 43 Welsh Guardsmen were killed. The decision to move the soldiers in daylight without proper air cover, and then leave them on board *Sir Galahad* for several hours, still arouses controversy. They were attacked by five Argentinian aircraft, and the *Sir Galahad* was immediately engulfed in stifling smoke and fire. Some of the guardsmen survived the inferno, but sustained horrifying burns. Nearly all these young men from Cardiff were either in their teens or early 20s, a reminder once more that it is youth that usually pays the price of war.

Between the two World Wars, 11 o'clock on 11 November was a moment when everything came to a standstill, as people stood in silent memory to pay homage to those who had made such an enormous sacrifice. After World War Two, ceremonies of remembrance were held on the nearest Sunday to 11 November, but recently the older tradition of two minutes silence on the actual day has returned. Every year the service held at the Welsh cenotaph is a deeply moving experience, but all the memorials from the wars of the 20th century are a poignant reflection of the suffering which such conflicts bring in their wake.

*The service at the Welsh National War Memorial every November is always a solemn and emotional scene as the suffering from the wars of the last 100 years is still remembered.*

**Further reading:**
**Chappell, E.L.** *Cardiff's Civic Centre*, Priory Press, 1946.
**Morgan, D.** *Cardiff, a City at War*, Dennis Morgan, 1998.

*Chapter 15*

# Where Broadcasting Began in Wales

Passers-by scarcely notice the tiny plaque on the wall of a shop at the junction of Castle Street and Womanby Street, yet it was in this building on 13 February 1923 that the BBC first began to broadcast to the people of Wales. The plaque was unveiled by Lord Reith on the 40th anniversary of that event. The Castle Picture Theatre occupied the premises in 1923, and the BBC's humble studio above the theatre, with a floor space of no more than 18 square feet, served as an office, a studio and a reception area. One early broadcast involved a male voice choir, an orchestra, with all its equipment, and an announcer. The conductor of the choir exhorted them to close up tightly, while telling them to take care in case they disappeared into Castle Street.

Two days before going on air, workmen were still trying to soundproof the studio with curtains and felt cloth. 'Drab as a warehouse and full of clutter', the furniture consisted of a few old chairs and a piano. Microphones, similar to old-

*In February 1923 a new medium of information, culture and entertainment was brought to the people of Wales. This little plaque at Black's Camping Shop in Castle Street reminds us where it all began.*

170

fashioned telephone ear pieces, hung from the ceiling. Programmes were transmitted via a Marconi transmitter based in the generating station at Eldon Road, or Ninian Park Road as it is known today. The chimney stack served as a support for the elevated wireless aerial.

Though the earliest listeners to programmes were restricted to the Cardiff area and the mining valleys to the north, the *Western Mail* was filled with enthusiasm for the new invention. 'Ethereal waves... will be picked up on aerials that flutter up in the air like clothes lines', wrote its enthusiastic reporter. He observed that aerials were springing up in all districts of the city, despite the fact that a receiver with valves could cost from £5 to £25. An alternative, costing just a few shillings, was the home-made crystal set. A licence fee of 10s was also obligatory, but the *Mail*, which carried numerous advertisements for new receivers and aerials, maintained that a wireless would give far better value than a gramophone. With its wires and earphones, the set resembled a contraption from science fiction and, to improve reception, the Post Office allowed customers to arrange up to 100 feet of rods and wires in their back gardens. Despite these measures, there were complaints in the early days of interference from amateur stations and shipping communications.

The opening broadcast began at 5pm on 13 February when Frederick Roberts, the station director, announced 'This is 5WA, the Cardiff Station of the British Broadcasting Company, calling'. Roberts's career ended prematurely the following

*Broadcasting had made enormous strides when Lord Reith unveiled this plaque on 13 February 1963. Though regional broadcasting was always given some latitude, it was Reith who set the standards that made the BBC a national institution.*

*One of the more expensive early wireless sets. With massive coils sliding into each other and an enormous amount of wire, there were those who queried the reason for calling it a 'wireless'.*

day when he was replaced by Rex Palmer after appearing tired and over-emotional in the studio.

The first programme was an hour of stories for children followed by an interval until 6.30pm. The seven-strong wireless orchestra then played *The Entry of the Gladiators* as an introduction to the official opening of the Cardiff station. John Reith, the man who guided the BBC in its early years, was present to introduce the guests. They included Lord Gainford, the chairman of the BBC, and Sir William Noble, one of its directors. Lord Gainford brought a message from Lloyd George, who expressed his satisfaction that Wales was taking part in 'this marvellous discovery'.

The Lord Mayor of Cardiff, Alderman J.J.E. Biggs, forecast that broadcasting would raise the standard of intellectual life, giving the poor 'the same opportunity as the people of Mayfair to hear the music of Paderewski and the voice of Melba'. With great foresight, he also prophesied that one day vibrations of light would be projected in the same way, allowing people to see 'the scenery, the architecture… and the paintings of Italy, Greece and Egypt'. The only hiccup in his speech came when he whispered in an aside heard by thousands 'What's the name of the organisation again?' The confined space at Castle Street only allowed two or three photographers and guests to be admitted at a time, but the Lady Mayoress invited a large company to the City Hall to hear the inaugural ceremony.

In the early years, programmes were produced by a few people who had no experience of broadcasting. A pioneer of those days observed that they were 'guardians and attendants of the most voracious creature ever created by man – a microphone which clamoured daily to be fed'. May Henderson, the 19-year-old secretary at the Cardiff station, found that her duties involved, 'searching the highways and byways for men and women who had the gifts of speech and song'. If the local talent, when asked to perform for the fledgling company, requested a fee she had to explain that there were no funds available for payment. The

*The guests at the opening ceremony made up a distinguished gathering. In this photograph are Lord Gainford, Sir William Noble, Sir R.W. Smith and John Reith, towering over everyone else.*

*Musical items played a major role in the entertainment chosen for the first evening. The baritone voice of Mostyn Thomas, supported by the Carston Quartette, seated next to the piano, was among the highlights.*

publicity to make a new reputation or enhance an old one was thought to be sufficiently rewarding. If no artistes were available, the tiny staff had to broadcast themselves. Rex Palmer sang in several programmes, using a different name each time. May Henderson's versatility showed itself when, as 'Auntie May', she read stories and played the piano in one of the BBC's most popular programmes, *Children's Hour*.

From its earliest days Welsh broadcasting was confronted with the problems of two languages and two countries. The Cardiff station was combined with Bristol to form the West region of the BBC and it was an unsatisfactory arrangement for everyone. Welsh speakers quickly realised that broadcasting offered a golden opportunity to promote the Welsh language, and they demanded a separate station for Wales with more programmes in Welsh. Nationalists claimed that 'the BBC administered Wales as a conquered province'. Listeners in the west of England complained that theirs was the only region of England 'inflicted with radio programmes in a foreign language'. Welsh people who only spoke English tended to agree. The *Western Mail* caustically observed 'Endeavouring to please both areas, the BBC only succeeded in displeasing both'. As the maximum range of 5WA was limited to 70 miles, many people could hear nothing in either language. A relay station came into service at Swansea in 1924, but not until 1935 was North Wales given a studio at Bangor.

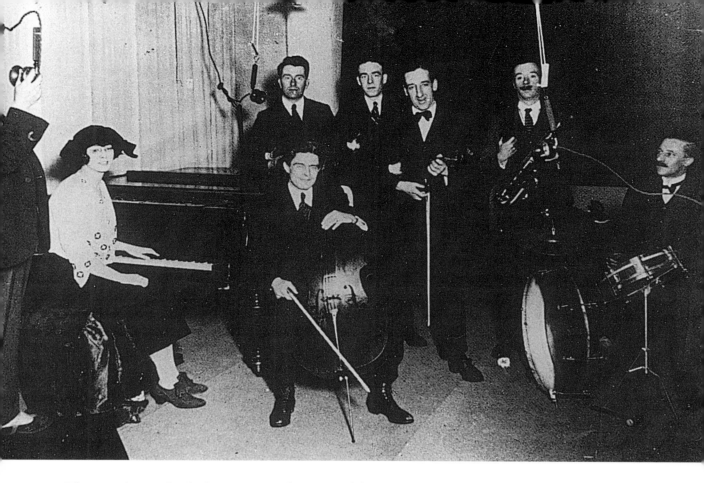

The premises at Castle Street were only occupied for just over a year, and in May 1924 Reith attended the official opening of what E.R. Appleton, director of the West Region, called 'my dream studio' in Park Place. In the early 1930s there were still only three full-time staff at the Park Place studios, but soon the BBC in Wales began to prosper, especially when Wales and the West became separate regions in 1937.

Many programmes reflected the views of John Reith that broadcasting should never be an 'organ of mere entertainment', but should provide 'all that is best in every department of human knowledge, endeavour and achievement'. Music was an important ingredient of entertainment on the wireless. The BBC Welsh Orchestra was formed in 1935 and all the great Welsh male voice choirs gave performances at different times. A feature on Sunday afternoons was the address given by leading clergymen in Wales. The earliest drama productions concentrated on the works of Shakespeare, but it was soon recognised that plays and talks, directed at an unseen listener, required writers who could write specifically for the wireless. Features such as 'Echoes of Old Cardiff' or 'The Chartist Riots' reflected Welsh history and culture.

Wynford Vaughan Thomas joined the Corporation as outside broadcasts assistant in 1936 and became a pioneer in the BBC's policy of vacating the studio and seeking programmes of interest in the heart of Wales. Increasing coverage was

*The first day's broadcasting came to an end with dance music and Welsh airs played by the Wireless Orchestra. Frederick Roberts, the announcer and first director of the station, who was replaced the next day, is on the left.*

*Park Place, the second home of the BBC in Wales. Originally only number 39 was occupied, but later 38 and 40 were acquired to provide extra space. Today the premises are used by the extra-mural department of the university.*

given to Welsh sport and Fred Keenor, the Cardiff City captain, made an early contribution when he gave his impressions of an international match between England and Wales.

Light entertainment included dancing to orchestras such as Waldini and his Gypsy Band, while Tessie O'Shea broadcast several times from the Empire in Cardiff. Mai Jones was the principal organiser of light entertainment, and it was she who produced *Welsh Rarebit*, probably the most famous of Welsh radio programmes. It was first broadcast in February 1940 to entertain British troops in France. There was a promise that the programme would contain a new song. That song, *We'll keep a welcome in the hillside*, was led by the Lyrian Singers and almost became a second Welsh national anthem. Maudie Edwards, Stan Stennett and Harry Secombe all took part in *Welsh Rarebit* at some stage in their careers. *Tommy Trouble*, a sketch written by E. Eynon Evans, was one of the highlights of the show. The mixture of comedy, music and hwyl was such that the programme, coming from the Cory Hall in Cardiff, ran for nearly 20 years.

When television came to Wales in 1952, the activities of the BBC increased enormously. There were echoes of 1923 as makeshift premises in a former Methodist chapel at Broadway in Cardiff became its first TV studio. A number of fine plays were produced there, including *The Corn is Green* and *How Green was my Valley*.

For some years the radio continued to be a more important service than television. The premises in Park Place had served the Corporation well for 40 years, but it was clear that BBC Wales needed much more spacious accommodation. In 1952 the Corporation acquired Baynton House, a mansion set

*Welsh Rarebit became such a favourite among listeners that it was broadcast nationally on the Light Programme. Tom Jones, E. Eynon Evans, Lyn Joshua and Phil Philips were the stars of the ever popular sketch* Tommy Trouble.

*Broadcasting House, the headquarters of BBC Wales, was officially opened by Princess Margaret on St David's Day, 1967. The buildings are now the principal studios for radio and television in Wales.*

*Black's Camping Shop 2005. The plaque, commemorating the first studio of the BBC in Wales, can be seen on the wall to the right hand side of the entrance to the shop.*

in 10 acres of land at Llandaff. On the 40th anniversary of broadcasting in Wales, building work began on the new studios in Llandaff, and they were first used in the autumn of 1966. The splendid headquarters of BBC Wales in Llantrisant Road are a far cry from those early days in Castle Street where the magic of the air waves were first heard in the Principality.

**Further reading:**

**Lucas, R.** *The Voice of a Nation*, Gomer Press, 1981.

# Index